Digital Scholarship

Routledge Studies in Library and Information Science

Digital Scholarship

Edited by Marta Mestrovic Deyrup

Routledge
Taylor & Francis Group
New York   London

First published 2009
by Routledge
711 Third Avenue, New York, NY 10017, USA

Simultaneously published in the UK
by Routledge
2 Park Square, Milton Park, Abingdon, Oxon OX14 4RN

Routledge is an imprint of the Taylor & Francis Group, an informa business

© 2009 Taylor & Francis

Typeset in Sabon by IBT Global.

Library of Congress Cataloging in Publication Data

Digital scholarship / edited by Marta Mestrovic Deyrup.
    p. cm.—(Routledge studies in library and information science ; 6)
Includes bibliographical references and index.
  1. Digital libraries—Case studies.   2. Libraries—Special collections—Electronic information resources.   3. Electronic information resources.   4. Library materials—Digitization.   5. Archival materials—Digitization.   6. Libraries and scholars.   7. Communication in learning and scholarship—Technological innovations.   I. Deyrup, Marta Mestrovic.
  ZA4080.D549 2009
  025.00285—dc22
  2008025184

ISBN10: 0-7890-3688-6 (hbk)
ISBN10: 0-203-88595-3 (ebk)

ISBN13: 978-0-7890-3688-9 (hbk)
ISBN13: 978-0-203-88595-6 (ebk)

Contents

Preface

Christine L. Borgman

This edited collection of papers on digital scholarship fills an important gap in the professional literature of libraries and archives. While much has been written of late on the need for digital scholarship in the humanities, the examples that exist are mostly written by and for scholars. These chapters are written by librarians and archivists, all of whom are actively engaged in building digital collections and are working closely with scholars and students. Professional advice and experience are offered, but more importantly, these authors have taken a step back from the immediate project to reflect more broadly on the challenges in establishing, maintaining, and servicing digital scholarship in the humanities.

In all fields, the availability of scholarly content in digital form makes possible new research questions and new methods. The humanities have benefited from the ability to digitize text and page images of historic documents, mine large corpuses of texts and other forms of records, and assemble widely dispersed cultural objects into common repositories for comparison and analysis. Once digitized, traditional scholarly content such as correspondence becomes much more valuable. Exchanges of letters can be examined by people, places, and themes, rather than just chronologically. Yet digitization alone is not enough. Careful assessments are required, such as whether to replicate orthography or modernize for consistency and whether to produce page images or searchable text or both.

Chapters in this collection offer a balanced view of the strengths and weaknesses of various approaches to digitization, and report both progress and problems. They examine new business models, new forms of partnerships, and new types of library and archival services that can be provided with these resources. The projects presented in this book have brought new audiences to old materials, thus enhancing humanistic scholarship for the digital age.

1 A Universal Humanities Digital Library

Pipe Dream or Prospective Future?

Shawn Martin

INTRODUCTION

According to Mary Sue Coleman, President of the University of Michigan, the Google digitization effort indicated "the global library was under way. It was no longer a question of 'whether' but rather 'how' and when.'"[1] This may be true in many respects, but, according to a recent survey by Martha Brogan, "while the texts of their trade are rapidly becoming available anywhere, anytime, humanities scholars, who might have much to gain from digital media's potential to spread their scholarship, remain firmly committed to traditional forms."[2] Later, Brogan cites the paucity of sustainable business models for the creation of electronic humanities scholarship, particularly in American literature, saying that "publishers and librarians alike look to models such as the TCP (Text Creation Partnership) as the only economically viable way to produce high-quality, thoroughly edited and encoded texts."[3] Therefore, it would appear that at least for the humanities, this dream of a universal digital library that Mary Sue Coleman envisions is little more than a pipe dream.

The TCP is certainly not the only business model that addresses the many problems of sustainable digital scholarship in the humanities. Projects like NINES (networked infrastructure for nineteenth-century electronic scholarship) at the University of Virginia, Women Writers' Online at Brown University, and the Humanities Text Initiative at the University of Michigan are all good examples of digital libraries in the humanities. However, all of these models are either grant funded, small, or are built for individual scholarly audiences.

Nonetheless, TCP is one of the largest and most successful models for the creation of digital libraries currently available. By looking at some of the lessons the TCP has learned over the past seven years of creating electronic text, it may be possible to see some of the characteristics that will be required to create future digital libraries for the humanities. What are some of these lessons? First, all large-scale digital humanities projects will probably need to fulfill research needs not currently met by existing resources. Second, they will need to collaborate in non-traditional ways with the commercial sector, elementary schools, museums, public libraries, and other similar institutions. Third, they will need to be decentralized among many institutions in order to create economies of scale. Fourth, they need to have clear but flexible procedures that allow for standardized workflow across all participating institutions. Fifth, they need to seek a middle ground. Rather than creating databases highly useful for very narrow audiences, projects should try to be useful to as many people as possible without becoming too general. Finally, all large-scale projects need to realize just how expensive an undertaking the creation of a large digital library is (probably millions of dollars over a period of years). In essence all of these lessons are a part of a bigger question, sustainability. All future digital libraries must be sustainable. The question is how. TCP may provide some insights into that problem.

BACKGROUND: THE TEXT CREATION PARTNERSHIP PROJECT

The TCP is unique in many ways. It does not utilize any grant funding for its primary operations. It collaborates with rather than competes against commercial publishers. It is extremely decentralized. The project utilizes several different interfaces because TCP collaborates with over twenty scholarly projects. The project gets its funding from over 150 institutions around the world, and though TCP is headquartered in an academic library, librarians at the project work closely with scholars to integrate TCP's resources into both the curriculum and research projects.

Why does TCP have this very unique model? It was founded for a specific purpose which so far has served it well.[4] In 1998 ProQuest Information and Learning was selling its product Early English Books Online (EEBO), a digitized version of its microfilm collection, which contains nearly every work printed in England between 1470 and 1700. There are roughly 125,000 titles and millions of images. The product allowed researchers to search catalog records from the old microfilm collections and immediately pull up digital images of the book. Though the libraries buying EEBO saw its obvious benefits, it was not really adding tremendously to their collections. After all, many of the large libraries in the United States already had access to EEBO in microfilm. So, although an electronic version was more convenient, it was not enhancing scholarship in any radical way.

One way to improve EEBO's utility to scholars, many thought, would be to add full text searchability. That way, a scholar could look up citations of particular authors, search for events in history like the Great Fire of London, or look for word patterns and how they changed over time. ProQuest too saw the potential benefit for creating such a collection, but thought that the cost in producing full text for the collection was too great. Because of the inadequacy of early fonts, OCR (Optical Character Recognition) technology that automatically creates text from digitized images would likely be too inaccurate to produce any meaningful results. The other option, having human beings type out the text, would be too expensive. So, therefore, ProQuest felt that the images, imperfect as they might be, would have to suffice.

Rather than taking no for an answer, the Universities of Michigan and Oxford believed there would be enough support from libraries to create text for at least part of the collection, and the TCP was born. Michigan and Oxford sought to create a partnership among libraries, scholars, and publishers that would help to serve the needs of all those communities as best as possible. That original effort has now expanded to two other products: Evans Early American Imprints (Evans), produced by Readex, and Eighteenth Century Collections Online (ECCO), produced by Gale. Together these three collections contain nearly every work printed in England and America between 1470 and 1800, around 300,000 titles. TCP endeavors to create texts for about 20 percent of the entire collection and to date has created around 18,000.

How is TCP text created? TCP text is created to a common standard across all three projects. Librarians at the TCP like to call what they do "TEI lite with additions." TEI (the Text Encoding Initiative) is a set of guidelines for the creation of e-text, particularly in the humanities. It has many different levels of encoding, the lowest being the basic structure of the text (things like paragraphs and chapters) and the highest being specific features meant for high level research (the syntax of sentences and typographical variants). TCP uses lower level tagging (TEI lite) but also adds some tagging for features that will obviously be of use to scholars, like typeface changes and colophons (with additions). TCP does this because it is trying to make as few editorial decisions as possible. It is hoped that TCP text can be used as a foundation that scholars can add to as needed for particular research projects.[5]

All texts TCP creates also are done to a 99.995 percent accuracy rating. Two people simultaneously type out the text. A third person then looks at both versions and corrects any discrepancies between the two versions. A fourth person (a staff member at Michigan or Oxford who has a background in early English/American history and literature) then reviews the text to see if there are any errors; if there are, it is sent back to be re-transcribed. In all, TCP texts are as accurate as can be created given the constraints that TCP faces such as poor quality in scanning of the microfilm and the need to produce texts in a most cost efficient manner.

Yet, when TCP is only creating text for a certain number of titles, and not the entire collection, how can people at the project possibly determine which texts are going to be of most benefit to the scholars and students of the future? This is where scholarly collaboration plays an important role. TCP has established task forces of relevant scholars who determine which texts should be selected out of the entire pool of nearly 300,000 titles.[6] Though, obviously the guidelines vary from project to project, there are certain similarities among all three. In all projects the TCP will only encode first editions unless there is a compelling scholarly reason to do otherwise (for example, the first edition is incomplete or missing pages, or a later edition is more representative of the multiple variations in a particular book). All projects use a foundational bibliography like the *New Cambridge Bibliography of English Literature* or the *Bibliography of American Literature*. No materials are excluded because they are contained in another project. Most importantly, TCP is dedicated to collaborating with the scholarly community to determine which titles it would like selected. Librarians from the TCP go to scholarly conferences, hold meetings about how texts are being used in research and in the classroom, and TCP works with an academic advisory group to keep TCP staff informed of general trends.[7]

How is it possible to fund this? Rather than using a grant-funding model more common among humanities projects, TCP has opted for a quasi-commercial model. In essence, once an institution (normally a university library, but also academic departments, special libraries and other institutions as well) purchases EEBO, Evans, or ECCO, it has an option of supporting the TCP. These institutional contributions are then matched by the commercial publishers and all of the money TCP collects is used to fund text production. Therefore, the more money TCP collects, the more texts it is able to produce, and the cost of each individual text becomes less expensive for the individual institutions supporting TCP. Currently TCP produces texts at a price of roughly two dollars per title for a large research university and even less for smaller liberal arts colleges.

Most importantly the TCP is more than just another commercial product. As an academic project, TCP is committed to the goals of open access, library ownership, protection of the public domain, and facilitating scholarly communication. Every text that TCP produces will eventually be released into the public domain and will become available to all institutions and individuals. How does TCP release text into the public domain? According to TCP's agreements with the three publishers, all text that TCP produces will remain available only to subscribers of the commercial product for a period of five years after production of text has ended. So, for instance, if the TCP project were to end now (in 2008), the three publishers would have the ability to sell their collection with TCP text until 2013; in 2013, any of the institutions that have access to TCP text are able to make that text publicly available, and many institutions already have plans in place to release the text once it does become available. This is a mutually beneficial arrangement because the libraries that pay for TCP text have the ability to make it accessible (though perhaps not as quickly as they would like), and publishers have the ability to enhance their product and sell those enhancements without any competition from freely available text. This allows the publishers to recoup the investments they have made in TCP through additional sales.

LESSONS LEARNED FROM THE TCP PROJECT

How is TCP relevant to digital scholarship in general? Although TCP does cater to a specific audience in early modern English and American studies, the students and scholars who use TCP include a cross section of many different scholarly disciplines (history, literature, law, linguistics, and science) and have a large range of technical expertise. So, even though TCP is limited to a specific group, it is a useful test case for other forms of scholarship as well. TCP is also the only project that collaborates with commercial publishers, libraries, and scholars on so large a scale. Therefore, it is possible to glean some lessons both from the audience and from the infrastructure that TCP has created over the past several years. Digital libraries of the future will need to meet needs not currently met by existing resources. They will need to collaborate with different kinds of partners not usually utilized in traditional grant models. They will need to be decentralized. They will need to have standardized procedures. They will need to try to seek a middle ground between high scholarly utility and general applicability, and they will need to find ways of creating enough capital to sustain operations on a large scale.

MEETING NEEDS NOT MET BY CURRENT ELECTRONIC RESOURCES

In the case of the TCP, there was no way that researchers could perform a full text search within individual titles of the EEBO collection. Clearly this was an important research need. Researchers might want to search people or places for a paper.

Students might want a more readable copy of early works to help them decipher difficult to read early gothic fonts. Librarians could wish to look for citations in a bibliography. Linguists will desire to look for word patterns in particular time periods. Literary scholars will need the ability to create electronic scholarly editions. Without TCP, those kinds of uses of the collection were impossible. Therefore, someone needed to step in and create the ability to utilize the collection for these advanced forms of research and teaching. TCP did so.

Once the searchable text was in place, another need for scholarly research within EEBO was to retrieve words regardless of their spelling. In early modern texts, spelling was not standardized and a search on "saint" would not find variant spellings like saynt, saynte, saynct or the like. Therefore, another project funded by the Committee on Institutional Collaboration (a consortium of the Big Ten Universities and the University of Chicago) headquartered at Northwestern University is mapping modern standardized spellings to their early modern variants. The Virtual Modernization project will soon be integrated into EEBO and allow more accurate searching within TCP texts.[8] So, in the same way that EEBO has allowed more kinds of academic use, Virtual Modernization will do the same by meeting a scholarly need currently unavailable in existing electronic resources.

The same is also true of the Evans and ECCO collections. Though one could argue that because of OCR text running behind the images in Evans and ECCO, a TCP project is not needed, it is also true that many kinds of research need the added value that TCP offers to encourage electronic scholarship. OCR is not always perfect in its accuracy. It does not contain structural tagging marking paragraphs on chapters needed for the creation of electronic scholarly editions. From a library perspective, it is also important to create a canon of electronic materials that can be used free of the constraints of intellectual property present in commercial collections.[9] TCP because of its policy to release all materials will allow universities that do not have access to collections like EEBO, Evans, or ECCO to eventually use them, thus meeting a need of faculty and students at smaller, less wealthy institutions.

NON-TRADITIONAL COLLABORATION

One of the unique, and more controversial, features of the TCP has been its collaboration with rather than competition against commercial publishers. This relationship stems from a mutual realization that commercial publishers need to change their models in the electronic environment and that university libraries are unable to create collections on the vast scale that commercial publishers can. Given the high cost of scanning, cataloging, maintaining, and producing a database with hundreds of thousands of titles, only publishers with vast amounts of capital can possibly create a collection the size of EEBO.

It is true that collaboratively universities have been able to do amazing things such as the Internet Archive run by Brewster Kahle. Nonetheless, the more institutions in a collaboration, the more difficult it gets to efficiently run an organization. A commercial publisher can decide to invest millions of dollars in a project, create it, and effectively get its money back in a timely fashion. Two hundred universities working together can invest comparable (though likely smaller) amounts over a longer period of time, create the product in a slow and meticulous fashion, and get its money back in intangible ways which are difficult to measure.

Commercial publishers are set up to produce digital libraries like EEBO quickly and cost effectively. Academic institutions are able to contextualize, understand, and add expertise to those libraries in ways that commercial publishers never could. Therefore, rather than competing with each other, it is important to cooperate. Though Michigan could have decided to independently create freely available texts with grants or institutional subscriptions, it likely would have produced less text and taken a longer time period. Similarly ProQuest, Readex, or Gale could have produced text more efficiently, but it likely would have been of little use to scholarship. Therefore, TCP attempts to capitalize on the strengths of both.

DECENTRALIZATION

Decentralization, particularly at Oxford, has allowed TCP to meet the differing needs of scholars in both the U.K. and the U.S. It has allowed the TCP to create a smaller collection of texts in languages other than English by utilizing the strengths that our partners like the University of Toronto have in Latin and other early modern dialects of modern languages or like the National Library of Wales has in Welsh language books. It has allowed departments with strengths in linguistics or other disciplines to advise the project on how to create texts that will be more useful for scholarship of the future. In essence, cooperation with such a diverse number of universities around the world has allowed TCP to cater to differing needs of the humanities community in ways that no centralized project could do.

Decentralization is, however, a double-edged sword. Though many institutions are involved, Michigan and Oxford are still the primary centers of the projects' efforts. The more universities that are involved, the more coordination is required to insure proper communication among various centers. The more coordination needed, the higher the overhead cost of administration becomes. The higher the overhead cost becomes, the more potential there is for inefficiency within the system. So it is a fine balance between decentralization and efficiency that TCP certainly struggles with but has effectively been able to manage over the past several years by encouraging other institutions to become part of the project, while at the same time trying to limit major operations to only two or three universities that have the most experience and expertise to manage projects like the TCP.

STANDARDIZATION

Another one of the ways that TCP has effectively been able to manage this decentralized structure is through standardization of workflows. All of the staff at the Universities of Michigan, Oxford, Toronto, the National Library of Wales, and other projects that cooperate with TCP adhere to the same principles of text creation. There is a standard way TCP creates text, a common philosophy under which we operate, and a standard editorial policy used for all texts TCP produces.[10] Also, all universities that cooperate with the TCP hold to a similar philosophical principle that understands the benefits of working with commercial publishers and realizes the importance of balancing priorities between commercial and academic interests. This philosophy is stated on the first page of the Web site:

The Text Creation Partnership (TCP) at the University of Michigan is bringing together the international library community with commercial scholarly publishers to support the creation of accurately keyboarded and encoded editions of thousands of culturally significant works in all fields of scholarly and artistic endeavor. The underlying principles of the TCP are mindful of the long-term needs of libraries, scholars and the larger society. TCP projects are notable for the quality and cost-effectiveness of their content, as well as for the underlying principles of the Partnership that:

• Convey robust rights of use to scholars;
• Protect the public domain rights of the larger society to access out-of-copyright materials;
• Present the user with accurately keyed, modern texts that are faithful to the spellings and organization of the original works;
• Ensure that this content will migrate forward through shifts in technology to represent editions of enduring value to libraries.

The net effect of the TCP initiatives has been to maximize the respective strengths of commercial and academic digital library development for the long-term benefit of researchers and students. [11]

FINDING A MIDDLE GROUND

The key to these constant struggles between collaboration and centralization or standardization and meeting individual needs has been TCP's desire to seek a middle ground between seemingly opposing directions. Many scholarly projects seek to create a highly edited and tagged corpus of material meant for a specific group of scholarly users. Though these projects unquestionably offer a better alternative for scholars in those disciplines, they also cost a great deal of money and produce a very small number of titles. TCP on the other hand produces many more texts than smaller-scale projects have done. Though it is true that TCP texts are done to a much lower standard and, therefore, are less useful to scholars than a highly tagged text would be, TCP does not aim to be a project useful to any particular group within the humanities community. Rather the project seeks to provide a foundation for other groups to build upon.

CREATING CAPITAL

One of the main problems all digital libraries face is money. It is incredibly important that all projects realize how expensive a digital library is to create. Just to use the figures of TCP, to complete 41,000 texts (approximately

20 percent of the entire collection in EEBO, Evans, and ECCO), will cost approximately $13,000,000. If TCP were to create text for the entire collection of roughly 300,000 texts it would cost over $100,000,000. These figures also do not count the ongoing costs of maintenance and preservation which will likely need to be borne by institutions in the future. Though TCP's costs are perhaps not applicable to all types of digital libraries, it does indicate that the cost of creating an electronic collection is higher than any grant, any single institution, or any combination thereof, is likely to be able to generate. Digital libraries of the future will need to generate large amounts of capital and will probably need to seek it among multiple institutions and from the commercial sector. TCP is just one way of doing this.

SUSTAINABILITY

In essence, all of these lessons TCP has learned about its own model for digital library creation are part of one fundamental question for digital scholarship in the humanities, sustainability. In order for a project to be sustainable it has to have enough money; in order to have enough money there needs to be a large enough audience to support a project monetarily; in order for there to be a large enough audience, there has to be a broad enough range of material to support such an audience; in order to create so broad a range of material, there needs to be a standardized procedure for creating it. TCP has been very successful in creating a broad range of material and standardized workflows, and has been largely successful in creating a large enough audience and collecting large amounts of money. The project still struggles with how to get greater support among libraries and the scholarly community and creating a business model that will allow the project to continue creating this middle ground between commercial publishers and the scholarly community.

WHAT DOES THIS MEAN FOR DIGITAL SCHOLARSHIP?

Daniel Pitti has argued that the key to creating sustainable projects and publications is collaboration and that "collaboration depends on sustainable project design . . . If a project is collaborative and if it is to succeed, it will require the attributes of standardization, documentation, and thoughtful, iterative design."[12] To a degree Pitti has come to many of the same conclusions that TCP has found through seven years of work. TCP has certainly learned that some of the secrets of its own success have been the collaborative, decentralized nature of the project, its cooperation with commercial publishers, its use of standards, its ability to enhance collections to make them more useful for scholars, and its ability to navigate a middle ground among many competing interests. Is it really sustainable?

Yes and no. What do the lessons of the TCP mean for the future of digital libraries in the humanities generally? They mean that TCP like many other projects will need to think about its role in new ways. The community involved in the creation of digital libraries will need to be more proactive. Digital libraries will need to reconsider the role of content and access. Finally, they will need to think about their roles even more broadly than they have done in the past.

Like Blanche DuBois in *A Streetcar Named Desire*, TCP has relied greatly on "the kindness of strangers." They have included the librarians who contribute monetarily to the project, the scholars and students who use the texts, the publishers who integrate them into their databases, the staff of other projects that have advised TCP on how to create text, and the staff of organizations like the Council on Library and Information Resources who help to contextualize TCP in larger frameworks. All of these groups have their own agendas and all have been proactive in promoting these agendas to the TCP. In turn, TCP has tried to accommodate as many of them as possible.

TCP has undoubtedly benefited from this input, but it like all projects needs to benefit more. Audiences for digital libraries need not only advance their agendas to TCP, they need to advance the agenda of the TCP to other groups. In other words, users of digital libraries need to tell others about the benefits of projects like TCP. They need to evangelize those who may still not understand. They need to be proactive in supporting models that they think are effective.

Second, digital libraries traditionally have merged the role of content and access to that content. In other words they create not only texts and images but also an entire database around that information so that it can be accessed in particular ways. Digital libraries of the future may need to separate those two functions. TCP seeks to create content that can be searched in DLXS (its own database system), Google, or any other system that searches text. On the opposite side of the spectrum, PhiloLogic, a database system developed at the University of Chicago particularly useful for linguistics research, searches texts of collections like TCP and multiple other publishers. Now the two work together. TCP creates content which PhiloLogic searches. PhiloLogic serves a particular scholarly community that searches TCP and other databases. Currently most humanities projects build both content and a system to search it. This often means that valuable content cannot be searched in other databases because it was never designed to do so. In the future, it may be better to either build content or access. That is, to build content (images, text, metadata) that can be searched by other systems or to build databases that can search multiple different kinds of content.[13]

Finally, and most importantly, communities that build and utilize digital libraries will need to think more broadly about their roles in the creation and dissemination of electronic scholarship. This could include collaborating with publishers, public libraries, museums, or schools. It might mean commercializing certain aspects of digital library creation. It might mean closing some content and selling it while at the same time opening up access to other information.

CONCLUSION

The question for consumers and producers of digital scholarship will be how to create an infrastructure that both disseminates ideas and attracts capital in the electronic age. Infrastructure by definition is "fundamentally characterized by access, 'shareability,' and economic advantage."[14] All three of these factors are important in thinking about how to create a cyberinfrastructure of digital scholarship: access to one's own ideas and those of others, ability to share those ideas with others, and economic benefits of sharing those ideas freely rather than paying for them. Though most scholarly projects provide access and shareability, they lack economic advantage. Though they may be highly useful to scholars in a narrow range of inquiry, they may be of dubious utility for scholarship in general. TCP would seem to have all three qualifications.

The recent report on cyberinfrastructure in the humanities stated that "in considering how best to organize the publishing side of scholarly communication, it will also be important to be open to new business models."[15] Mary Sue Coleman also said that:

> Society turns to its universities for the printed word because books are the foundation of our institutions. Books are what the first president of Michigan called our 'fixed capital,' more vital than any professor, any classroom, or any laboratory. We are the repository for the whole of human knowledge, and we must safeguard it for future generations. . . . We want all scholarly communication to succeed. And that is because of the vital importance, and the integral role, that publishing plays in the academy.[16]

The TCP provides some possibilities for building digital "fixed capital" for the academic community. It is one possible model for moving into this future that the Commission on Cyberinfrastructure and Mary Sue Coleman envision. A universal digital library is not a pipe dream, but a prospective and a necessary future. Nonetheless it is a future that has a long way to go and requires the dedicated work of many people thinking in new and creative ways about their work.

NOTES

1. Mary Sue Coleman, "Google, the Khmer Rouge, and the Public Good," (address to the Association of American Publishers, February 6, 2006 http://

www.umich.edu/pres/speeches/060206google.html (accessed September 8, 2007).

2. Martha Brogan, *A Kaleidoscope of Digital American Literature*, Digital Library Federation and Council On Library and Information Resources (September, 2005), 7.

3. Ibid., 29.

4. Much has already been written about the Text Creation Partnership. For more information see Mark Sandler, "New Uses for the World's Oldest Books: Democratizing Access to Historic Corpora," *ARL Bimonthly Report* 232 (February 2004): 4–6 and Shawn Martin, "Collaboration in Electronic Scholarly Communication: New Possibilities for Old Books," *Journal of the Association for History and Computing.* IX, no. 2 (October 2006) http://mcel.pacificu.edu/jahc/2006/issue2/martin.php.

5. More information about the technical details of the texts can be found at http://www.lib.umich.edu/tcp/eebo/proj_des/pd_wgrouprecs.html.

6. Minutes of these task forces can be found at http://www.lib.umich.edu/tcp/eebo/proj_stat/ps_tstaskforce.html and http://www.lib.umich.edu/tcp/eebo/News/Task_Force_Report.html.

7. A list of the members of the academic advisory group can be found at http://www.lib.umich.edu/tcp/eebo/proj_stat/aag.html.

8. More detailed information about the Virtual Modernization project can be found at http://www.lib.umich.edu/tcp/eebo/News/Newsletter-01–06.pdf and at http://www.library.northwestern.edu/collections/garrett/TCP_Virt-Mod.ppt.

9. For more information on the problems of OCR texts, particularly as they relate to Evans and ECCO, see Shawn Martin, "Digital Scholarship and Cyberinfrastructure in the Humanities: Lessons from the Text Creation Partnership," *Journal of Electronic Publishing* X, no. 1 (Winter 2007) http://hdl.handle.net/2027/spo.3336451.0010.105.

10. These policies are available at http://www.lib.umich.edu/tcp/docs/. Keep in mind that these are working documents not meant to produce a standard per se. Rather, they are constantly evolving ways of thinking as staff at the TCP find new problems.

11. Available at http://www.lib.umich.edu/tcp (accessed September 8, 2007).

12. Daniel Pitti, "Designing Sustainable Projects and Publications," in *A Companion to the Digital Humanities*, eds. Susan Schreibman, Ray Siemens, and John Unsworth (Oxford: Blackwell Publishing, 2004), 487.

13. Many projects are already trying to build tools that search multiple kinds of information, for more see Bernie Frischer et. al., *Summit on Digital Tools for the Humanities: Report on Summit Accomplishments* (Charlottesville: University of Virginia, 2006).

14. Amy Friedlander, *Power and Light: Electricity in the U.S. Energy Infrastructure 1870–1940* (Reston: Corporation for National Research Initiatives, 1996), 6.

15. John Unsworth et. al., *Our Cultural Commonwealth: The Report of theAmerican Council of Learned Societies' Commission on Cyberinfrastructure for the Humanities and Social Sciences* (Washington, D.C.: American Council of Learned Societies, 2006), 32 http://www.acls.org/cyberinfrastructure/acls.ci.report.pdf (accessed September 8, 2007).

16. Coleman (see note 1).

2 The "Russian Doll Effect"

Making the Most of Your Digital Assets

James Bradley

INTRODUCTION

When I consider the short history of digital librarianship, I cannot help but reference this small piece of family folklore:

> Several years ago, my father was piloting a carload of family members through northern Kentucky en route to a Cincinnati Reds baseball game. Crossing the apex of a large hill, all the passengers were unhappy to see a double line of motionless cars and trucks on the road ahead. Reacting quickly, perhaps instinctively, my father avoided the traffic jam by slowing down and turning onto a smaller side road. My uncle, alarmed at the sudden route change, exclaimed, "We're going the wrong way!" To which my adventurous father replied, "True, but we're making *very good time!*"

The advent of the World Wide Web in the early 1990s[1] ushered in a new paradigm for libraries. The graphic nature of the Web, combined with simple searching tools, allowed the general populace to access information quickly and with very little technical knowledge.

Some librarians saw the internet as a threat, others as an opportunity. Either way, there was mounting pressure for academic and public libraries to generate an online presence to compete amongst the growing number and popularity of Web-based information sources. This urgent need to produce online content, coupled with a lack of logistical standards for its construction, forced many librarians and information professionals to make the same choice my father did: to move forward, even if it was perhaps in the wrong direction.

These early projects largely produced "silos"—digital objects marooned within a set of static HTML Web pages. This model was somewhat improved through database-driven "dynamic" Web sites; however, digital collections remained highly localized and idiosyncratic until the development of dedicated content management systems (CMS), specialized metadata sets (e.g.,

Dublin Core, MODS, METS), and widely-accepted exchange protocols (e.g., OAI-PMH).

With these technologies now in place, we are experiencing a renewed push to create new content; however, in the rush to create digital content, we must resist the urge to simply create a glut of electronic artifacts without considering the short-term and long-term possibilities of objects' usage. In the Web 2.0 world, a well-planned digital artifact will find itself repurposed and repackaged several times for a variety of environments, gateways, and diverse user types—a phenomenon I have begun referring to as the *"Russian Doll Effect."*

In this chapter, I would like to explore the flexibility of digital objects accommodating simultaneous usage in multiple contexts, illuminating the discussion through a series of specific examples drawn from Ball State University's Digital Media Repository (http://libx.bsu.edu).

BALL STATE UNIVERSITY'S DIGITAL MEDIA REPOSITORY

In February 2005, Ball State University Libraries launched its Digital Media Repository with a single collection of 982 photographic images. The DMR has continued to grow steadily, with thirty-two collections available at the time of this writing, comprised of more than 80,000 individual objects.

The Digital Media Repository was the first online project at Ball State that utilized a "turnkey" content management system,[2] which allowed for both a rapid expansion of digital materials, and instant compatibility with OAI harvesters. Prior to the establishment of the DMR, there were a number of digital collections created by University Libraries, most notably the Ball State University Virtual Press[3]; and, while it remains a richly populated and extremely useful resource, it does illustrate the earlier "data silo" approach to online collections—a variety of digital objects locked within a static Web page architecture.[4]

In general, the collections within the Digital Media Repository were designed to fall within a handful of categories:

Reusable Learning Objects

The primary purpose of the Digital Media Repository was to house reusable learning objects that could be utilized in the classrooms at Ball State University. Examples of this type of collection are the Architecture Image Collection[5] and the Anatomical Model Collection.[6]

K–12 Educational Materials

Although some of the reusable learning objects we created had to be limited to the Ball State University community due to copyright restrictions or licensing agreements, we found that some materials could be offered freely to any classroom with an Internet connection. With this revelation, we targeted some collections for primary and secondary schools, such as offering World War II era newsreels and films as streaming video,[7] or a large collection of letters, documents, photographs, and artifacts of the United States Civil War.[8]

A Showcase of Student Achievement

We also wanted to use the Digital Media Repository as a showcase for work produced by Ball State University students, thus allowing our graduates to quickly assemble an online portfolio of their accomplishments. Examples of these types of collections are the Student Art Collection[9] and the Student Filmmakers Collection.[10]

Local and Regional Community Resources

The Digital Media Repository could also be used as a hosting platform for community resources by partnering with local and regional groups and organizations that would otherwise lack the ability or the budget to create and maintain an online presence. For example, Ball State University Libraries worked with *The Muncie Times*, a regional African-American newspaper, to create an archive of its complete historic and current issues.[11] Preservation of the newspaper in this manner also allowed this small newspaper to become part of the Library of Congress' National Digital Newspaper Program.

Rare, Unique, or Special Interest Archival Collections

Finally, the Digital Media Repository could be used to house inimitable collections, providing access to unique and possibly fragile artifacts that were of historic or academic interest. Collections of this type include miniature furniture created under a work relief program initiated by the Works Progress Administration[12], a wide variety of oral history projects[13], and an assortment of newspaper articles, photographs, and other documents related to the production and filming of a 1915 silent movie (as well as streaming video of the film itself).[14]

THE "RUSSIAN DOLL EFFECT"

As stated previously, the collections within the Digital Media Repository were designed to fall within these categories; however, as we studied the interaction of the users with the DMR, we found that our collections were not solely attracting our targeted user group, nor were they being utilized in the manner we originally intended. In many cases, the usage patterns suggested that our collections were (or distressingly, were not) satisfying an unforeseen user need.

In further exploring the concept of the "Russian Doll Effect," I would identify three major types of contextual transformation, demonstrating each type through the evolution of specific Digital Media Repository collections.

Recontextualizing an Original Object

The Ball State University Department of Theatre and Dance contacted University Libraries with an interest in creating a collection for the Digital Media Repository. The Theatre Costume Shop had secured a grant to create, index and photograph the hundreds of costumes designed and created by students for various stage productions. The original grant was simply to create an internal searchable database of costumes that would act as a finding aid.

Early in the development of the collection, it was decided that we should photograph the costumes during the process, thus creating a visual record to accompany the finding aid. We also resolved to make the collection available to the public as a showcase of student work; however, by making this a public collection, we created a previously unforeseen manner of usage.

For years, the department (and in particular, the theatre costume shop) had sporadically rented materials to outside organizations. The Theatre and Dance Costume Collection made it possible to provide an online visual catalog of all costumes. Rental information could appear alongside the costumes, allowing prospective thespians to search the costumes through a variety of data points: costume description, sizing information, style, period, associated plays/characters, etc. Thus, placed in a new context, the collection provided a rather novel entrepreneurial opportunity and a subsequent source of income for the Department of Theatre and Dance.

Several of the Digital Media Repository collections have made similar contextual adjustments. For example, the Student Artwork Collection mentioned earlier in this chapter was originally intended to provide a quick and easy way for students in the Visual Arts program to assemble a portfolio of their artwork for grant applications, exhibition proposals, etc. However, in practice, we found that the faculty were accessing and utilizing the collection at a similar (and sometimes higher) rate.

Investigating this unanticipated usage pattern, we discovered that the student artworks were being called up by instructors for classroom use—spurring creativity in current students by demonstrating how previous students had interpreted and completed a particular assignment. We also learned that the collection had become an important marketing tool for the Department of Art by displaying the quality of works created within the department and assuring prospective students an online presence and electronic portfolio.

Thus, like a handful of nesting dolls, one contained within another, a single collection finds itself contextually reassigned. Originally conceived as a simple student tool, it transforms into a repository of reusable learning objects, a ready-made index of images for marketing purposes, a recruitment tool for new students, and (over time) a documentation of stylistic and artistic trends.

Additionally, we found that the collection has been added to wikis, blogs, and embedded and shared by the students themselves through social networking Web sites, which brings us to the next type of recontextualization.

Repurposing an Object within a Secondary Object

When partnering with Ball State University's Science–Health Science Library in the planning of the Anatomical Model Collection[15], we hoped that by creating digital facsimiles we could increase access to and extend the usable lifespan of the models. We meticulously photographed the models from various angles and even compiled some into three-dimensional QTVR objects, thereby allowing the user to grab the "virtual model," rotate it to any angle, and zoom in on any feature.

We were somewhat puzzled when the collection did not initially cultivate users, and circulation of the physical models remained relatively unchanged. Subsequent investigations revealed that although the students enjoyed having the models online, they were disappointed that the online collection did not contain a study guide for the models. Although we had faithfully recreated the model itself, we did not label the individual features of the model in a manner that would facilitate in-depth study.

Subsequent to this discovery, we worked with the Science-Health Science Librarian to repurpose the existing digital objects and to reuse them within annotated study guides that may be downloaded and printed. Further, we continue to solicit guidance from the faculty, to ensure all artifacts and study guides are relevant to class syllabi.

Learning from this experience, we began to envision other possible ways to reuse our existing digital artifacts within other secondary objects. The resulting project is the upcoming Ball State Teacher's Bookshelf.

Participants from various Ball State academic departments, (as well as from Ball State's Burris Laboratory School and the Indiana Academy) lend their knowledge and expertise within a specific discipline to the project by identifying objects within the Digital Media Repository and embedding them within "ready to go" instructional packets, which include source materials, lesson plans, handouts, quizzes, and study guides. Contributors from Ball State's School of Education and the Teachers' College then work to ensure these materials conform to state and federal curriculum guidelines and are assigned to appropriate age, grade, or developmental levels.

For example, the photographs, documents, letters, and artifacts already contained within the previously mentioned United States Civil

War Collection could be recontextualized and embedded within a four-week lesson plan appropriate for a seventh grade history class.

The end result of all this effort would call upon (and call attention to) the original resources of the Digital Media Repository, while at the same time creating a repository of freely available and openly downloadable "Reusable Learning Object Packets" for K–12 teachers in Indiana and beyond.

Planning Multiple Contexts for Emerging Technologies

From its inception, the Digital Media Repository has offered video produced by Ball State University. In addition to the Student Filmmakers Collection mentioned earlier, the DMR provides streaming video via the WIPB Documentary Video Collection[16], the Commencement Video Collection[17], the Robert F. Kennedy Speech Collection[18], and a handful of other projects; however, the advent of digital television, and the future need for multicontextual compatibility, caused us to completely reexamine the role of video assets within the DMR.

High Definition (HD) television sets were the top selling item of this past holiday season. A few well-researched consumers seemed to navigate the new technology with ease; yet, many of us were left silently pondering the difference between aspect ratios, debating 1080i against 1080p, and contemplating the merits of LCD versus rear projection, or versus plasma.

The digital television revolution has begun, and unlike other revolutions, this one has a definite end date: TV stations serving all United States markets are airing digital television programming today, although most will continue to provide analog programming through February 17, 2009. At that point, full-power TV stations will cease broadcasting on their current analog channels, and the spectrum they use for analog broadcasting will be reclaimed by the F.C.C. and put to other uses.

With digital television comes the need for digital storage. No longer will television stations be maintaining and storing programs on tapes. Digital video will instead be stored electronically, creating the need for a method of encoding for search and retrieval—the traditional point of expertise of the librarian.

In 2003, at WGBH-TV in Boston, librarians and information scientists from Rutgers University, the Department of Defense, and other institutions, combined efforts with broadcasting professionals from the Corporation for Public Broadcasting. The goal was to create a data set that would satisfy the needs of a television broadcaster while also remaining compatible with existing international library standards. The end result of this initial two-year project was the development of the PBCore (Public Broadcasting Core Data Elements), a metadata set specifically created to manage digital video assets.[19]

The PBCore is built on the foundation of the Dublin Core—the same metadata standard embedded within the CONTENTdm CMS which drives

Ball State University's Digital Media Repository. PBCore's hierarchical nature is a translation challenge for the flat file database required for CONTENTdm; however, the Corporation for Public Broadcasting suggests that a full PBCore record will not be necessary—or indeed practical—for most video assets, and encourage scalability within any local PBCore implementation. Therefore, for the purposes of the present Ball State WIPB-3 Video Project, it will be far more logical to develop a CONTENTdm metadata schema that will:

- Satisfy the needs of the current Digital Media Repository.
- Meet the current and anticipate the future needs of WIPB as a public television broadcaster.
- Be mapped to Dublin Core Elements for OAI-PMH compatibility.
- Be mapped to Qualified Dublin Core sets (such as PBCore) via XML/XSLT.

Thus, the Digital Media Repository's upcoming WIPB-3 Video Collection must fulfill the internal need to store and locate broadcast video content, while also delivering these assets as internet-based "video on demand" to a diverse set of users, through a variety of gateways, and to a wide array of entertainment devices. For this reason, the WIPB-3 Video Collection is the first collection we have created specifically to house multiple artifact versions to facilitate simultaneous multicontextual use (see diagram on following page).

SUMMARY AND CONCLUSIONS

If we redefine digital librarianship as digital stewardship, we take upon ourselves the mission to create and manage digital objects that are adaptable and sustainable over the longest period possible. Accordingly, we must assume that today's digital objects will be subject to the "Russian Doll Effect"—being utilized outside of their original context, repurposed and embedded within secondary environments, and accessed by a diverse user group using a variety of ever-changing information pathways and technologies. Creating digital artifacts with the inherent flexibility to meet these challenges is not an easy task, but it is not an impossible one. Although the road ahead is uncertain, there are actions we can take to ensure highly adaptable digital collections:

Scan Big

We can only assume that processing speeds, monitor resolutions, and bandwidths will continue to grow larger; thus (although it may seem like overkill by today's standards) digitizing objects at the highest level possible with

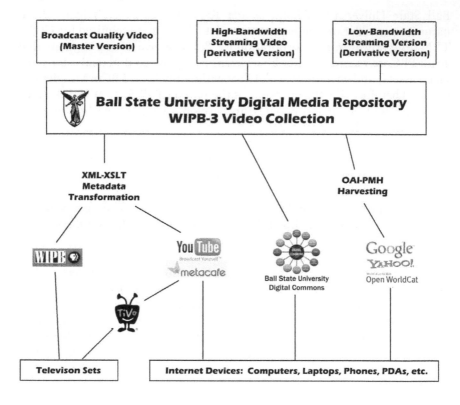

Figure 2.1   Multicontextual Asset Delivery.

current technology will hold off the inevitable obsolescence of the digital object for the longest possible term. Digitization at this level will require a lot of storage space, but this cost is justified when compared to the trouble and expense of re-scanning the original artifact.

Learn XML

The common denominator of all existing and emerging metadata sets is an Extensible Markup Language (XML) structure. XML was specifically designed to facilitate the sharing of data across different information systems, allowing for the quick and simple mapping and translation of one data standard to another through Extensible Stylesheet Language Transformations (XSLT). Becoming familiar with XML and its surrounding technologies is perhaps the best way to ensure your metadata (and thus your digital object) will survive recontextualization.

Know Your Users

As we have seen, although we begin a digitization project with a targeted group of users in mind, the collection may fail to satisfy their needs. It is therefore important to encourage a truly reflexive relationship with your intended audience (or, in the event of a partnership, your collaborators)—maintaining an open dialogue and updating the collection in accordance to documented needs. Additionally, examining the server statistics and Web analytics of your collection will allow you to identify unexpected user groups or usage patterns.[20]

Monitor Emerging Technologies

New technologies must always be monitored when building digital collections. Any technological advancement could have an effect on the digitization standards, best practices, and metadata planning. Moreover, since we assume all digital objects and systems will eventually become obsolete, familiarity with emerging technologies will aid in the early development and planning of artifact migration.

NOTES

1. More specifically, the release of the Mosiac/Netscape Web browser in 1994, Microsoft's Internet Explorer in 1995, and the numerous search engines that launched between 1993 and 1995 (e.g., WebCrawler, Lycos, Infoseek, AltaVista, Excite, etc.). Although networked computers and electronic messaging had been in existence for decades, its use was limited to a specialized minority.
2. In our case, CONTENTdm.
3. The Ball State University Virtual Press is available online at http://www.bsu.edu/library/virtualpress/.
4. In a step to improve the "silo" nature of these earlier online collections, Ball State University Libraries recently gathered together a variety of Web-based resources into the "Digital Commons" http://www.bsu.edu/libraries/viewpage.aspx?SRC=./lits/commons/index.html and is progressing toward "unlocking" the content within these sources via a federated gateway.
5. A representative sampling of more than 119,000 slides relating to architecture, landscape architecture, urban planning, and, to a lesser extent, art. Available online at http://libx.bsu.edu/collection.php?CISOROOT=%2FBSU_ArchSlidesCpght.
6. http://libx.bsu.edu/collection.php?CISOROOT=%2FAnatMod.
7. The World War II Historic Film Collection, available at http://libx.bsu.edu/collection.php?CISOROOT=%2FWWIIHistFilm. In addition to footage of campaigns in Europe and in the Pacific, the films document activities on the home front, including the efforts of African American colleges and farmers, the relocation and internment of Japanese civilians, and the victory garden program sponsored by the U.S. Office of Civilian Defense.

8. U.S. Civil War Resources for East Central Indiana available at http://libx. bsu.edu/LSTA/lstacivwar.php. This collection was funded by a Library Services and Technology Act grant and was created in partnership with a variety of institutions. For more on this collection, refer to the chapter in this volume written by John Straw.

9. Available in the Ball State Virtual Art Gallery, at http://libx.bsu.edu/collection.php?CISOROOT=%2FBSUArtists.

10. http://libx.bsu.edu/collection.php?CISOROOT=%2FBSStuFlm.

11. This collection consists of digitized volumes of the *Muncie Times* newspaper published by owner and publisher Bea Morten-Foster since the first issue in 1991. This bi-weekly publication serves the African American communities of Muncie, Richmond, Marion, New Castle and Anderson, Indiana. The Muncie Times Online Collection is available at: http://libx.bsu.edu/collection.php?CISOROOT=%2FMunTimes.

12. The miniature furniture was created between 1938 and 1942 as part of a unique work relief program initiated by the Works Progress Administration Indiana State Museum Project. The online collection is available at http://libx.bsu.edu/collection.php?CISOROOT=%2FMinFur.

13. The Middletown Digital Oral History Collection was funded by a Library Services and Technology Act grant and consists of audio and accompanying transcriptions for oral history interviews conducted with African American, Jewish and Catholic communities of Muncie, Indiana and local labor union leaders. It is available online at http://libx.bsu.edu/MidOrHist/midorhist.php.

14. *The Man Haters* is a rare 35mm silent movie filmed in Muncie, Indiana in 1915. The film was produced by Basil McHenry, a traveling film producer from Akron, Ohio. The digital collection is available at http://libx.bsu.edu/collection.php?CISOROOT=%2Fmnhtrs and contains the ten minute original version and a longer documentary version of *The Man Haters* film, newspaper clippings, photographs, and an essay about history of the film.

15. See note 5 above.

16. Available at http://libx.bsu.edu/collection.php?CISOROOT=%2FWIPBVid.

17. Available at http://libx.bsu.edu/collection.php?CISOROOT=%2Fcommence.

18. Available at http://libx.bsu.edu/collection.php?CISOROOT=%2FRFKen.

19. View the PBCore metadata set and related information at http://www.pbcore.org/.

20. Gathering information and usage patterns can be as simple as conducting informal interviews or usability testing. Another approach is to gather and examine the usage statistics of your online collection, a process known as "Web analytics." Web analytics allow you to learn more about who is using your collection, when they are accessing it, what queries they make to search the system, and what objects they access. To learn more about Web analytics in relation to an online collection (or more specifically CONTENTdm), read: Wibowo, P. Budi, "Discovering More Information About Your CONTENTdm Users Using W3C Format or Google Analytics," *Library Insider 5*, no. 2 (2007): 2. Available online at: http://libx.bsu.edu/cdm4/item_viewer.php?CISOROOT=/LibInsider&CISOPTR=79&CISOBOX=1&REC=43. Or, Wibowo, P. Budi, "How to Implement Google Analytics in a CONTENTdm System" *Library Insider 5*, no. 7 (2007): 6. Available online at: http://libx.bsu.edu/cdm4/item_viewer.php?CISOROOT=/ LibInsider&CISO PTR=84&CISOBOX=1&REC=48.

3 The Lives of Others
Editing Electronic Editions of Correspondence

Susan Schreibman

BACKGROUND

The editing of correspondence has had a long if somewhat repetitive history. From the earliest editions published in the eighteenth century to the most recent, editors have been struggling with issues of how best to present the text to a contemporary readership. Edited editions seek to add value beyond that which can be realized by publishing an image or facsimile of the original witness. The added value of these editions typically comes in the form of a critical introduction and annotation. Added value, more contentiously, comes in the form of editorial interventions to the text. These interventions are made for a variety of reasons. Sometimes they are carried out when portions of the text are excised at the behest of the family, executors, or the judgment of the editor. Interventions are also made to "improve" readability, for example by modernizing a text, by correcting obvious mistakes (of spelling for example), or to add or alter punctuation. Still other interventions come in the form of adjudication: if that mark above a letter in a word in French is an accent, although the correspondence typically does not add accents when handwriting text; or whether in print editions line breaks, spaces between section breaks, or font choice is meaningful. "In making explicit what in the physical text was implicit, the editor is inevitably providing a subjective interpretation of the meaning-bearing aspects of text. A later editor, or the same editor returning with new information, may disagree with an earlier interpretation."[1]

Scholarly editions of correspondence are generally reserved for the most famous: like all scholarly editions they are expensive to produce. Particularly in the case of recently deceased correspondents, the sensitivity of the content gives pause to trustees and heirs who would prefer not to have family secrets or insensitive remarks made widely available. For much of the twentieth century the editing of correspondence did not follow the same practice as literary editing. In the decades after the Second World War, editorial practice in the field of literature had been to restore a text to a state that most closely mirrored authorial intention. This was achieved by taking into consideration a variety of witnesses (first printing, later printings authorized by the author, original manuscript, etc.) to create an eclectic or "best text" edition. The resultant texts created an edition that never existed in the author's lifetime but would have been published (or could have been published) had there not been corruption introduced into the publishing process by copyeditors, editors, family members, and, sometimes, the author himself (here, the first printing of James Joyce's *Ulysses* is a case in point). Thus, the work of the literary editor was to compare, collate, and adjudicate so that the best text could be made available to the public.

Over the past fifteen years, there have been many critics of this method, arguing that many published works, increasingly so in the twentieth century, were the result of collaboration. Many writers expected their publishers to alter their texts (for example, to correct spelling or fix punctuation) and would be horrified to find a text restored to manuscript form. Thus, the theory of social text editing presumes that published words are collaborative acts between writers and any number of agents: editors, family members, friends—even critics. Contemporary textual scholars also argue that the physical artefact that carries a work is a contributory factor in how we interpret it. These physical features, manifested in book design and typography, the paper a letter was written on, the typewriter used for composition, the surrounding articles and advertisements of an article published in a newspaper, are meaning-carrying agents referred to as bibliographic codes.

Documentary editing, on the other hand, developed a set of practices to publish texts typically not intended for publication: letters, diaries, and journals. Frequently these exist only as one version or "witness": even in cases in which there is more than one witness, for example, when a letter writer kept a carbon copy or draft, the most authoritative version of the text, the letter that was actually posted or published, can be established.[2] The tradition of documentary editing for print publication has been to present the text as accurately as possible. This meant interpreting stray marks. Sometimes, depending on the goals of the edition, this results in correcting punctuation and unorthodox or incorrect spellings. Many documentary editions also preserve deletions while indicating insertions via superscript or subscript to help readers to follow the author's train of thought. These edited editions are typically augmented by scholarly apparatus—annotation, biographical notes, and introductory material. Making the correspondence of historical figures publicly available, particularly in the case of heads of state, is seen as a valuable addition to the historical record.

No matter what theory of textuality an editor subscribes to (if he has one at all), making available what are essentially private texts brings its own editorial challenges. These challenges have stayed remarkably constant over the last two and a half centuries. From one of the earliest editions of correspondence, *Letters to and from the Late Samuel Johnson, LL.D.*, published in 1788 by Hester Lynch Piozzi, to more recent editions, editors exert editorial privilege by correcting, altering, and eliminating text. Piozzi would be echoed throughout the centuries when she wrote:

An Editor's duty is indeed that of moft danger and leaft renown through all the ranks of literary warfare; all merit is attributed (and juftly) to the author; for faults, the perfon who publifhes muft be refponfible[3].

This short passage demonstrates one editorial decision. Do I modernise the use of the character *f* (typical of eighteen-century print publications) where we now use *s*. When silently altering the text so that it is in keeping with twentieth-first century practice, it also loses something which a reader reading the original publication would have access to: a sense of antiquity, of entering into another time which had different orthographic practices than our own.

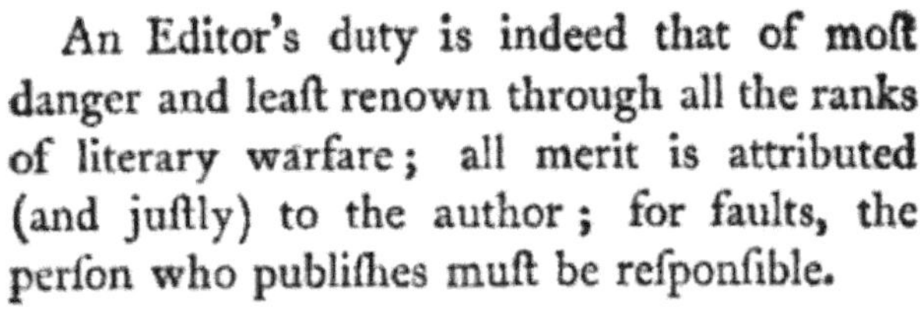

An Editor's duty is indeed that of moft danger and leaft renown through all the ranks of literary warfare; all merit is attributed (and juftly) to the author; for faults, the perfon who publifhes muft be refponfible.

Figure 3.1   The same passage as above from Piozzi's introduction to *Letters to and from the Late Samuel Johnson, LL.D.*

Later in her introduction, Piozzi takes pains to convey that the letters "remain juft as he worte them,"[4] although R.W. Chapman's 1952 three-volume edition of Johnson's letters reject all but four of Piozzi's letters as not genuine, either wholly or in part.[5] Piozzi does hint at why she may have altered some of the letters: "I have however been attentive to avoid paining many individuals, even for the gratification of that Public to which I am much more obliged."[6] This same reason is given by many contemporary editors, particularly when the published letters are near in time to their original authorship. Family members and friends of writers are no less sensitive in the twenty-first century than in the eighteenth to the potential damage to reputations.

There are also other tensions in how best to make correspondence available to a wide readership. Some in the archive community advocate that the best way to make widely available documentary materials is via facsimiles.[7] Over the past quarter of a century, facsimiles have typically been made available as part of a preservation microfilming project. Due to high printing costs, they have been published much more rarely in print. Sometimes this means of distribution is referred to as un-editing. Some of the arguments as to the relative merits of edited editions vs. unedited texts have to do with issues of preservation, of making cultural historical materials available to a wider audience, and of the best ways of helping contemporary audiences understand the past. Here, we might do well to remember that the aims of our transcriptions, and by extension our editions, may not be to represent the original as accurately as possible, but "rather to prepare from the original text another text so as to serve as accurately as possible certain interests in the text."[8]

ENTER THE DIGITAL

Digital editions have the ability to meld these different editorial practices. Presenting an edition of letters in an online edition which marries documentary practice with theories of social text editing provides opportunities for readers to access the bibliographic codes of the original documents, while taking advantage of the scholarship contained in the scholarly apparatus and text encoding. The economics of digital publication are also different. What was economically prohibitive in print (such as publishing facsimiles) is trivial in electronic editions. Moreover, the text encoding used by most scholarly editions not only provides access to the linguistic features of a document, it provides a vehicle for scholarly editing in which proper names can be normalized to facilitate searching (although proper names are not necessarily normalized for display purposes), annotation can be anchored within the text, and bibliographic information, such as the provenance of letters and methods for dating can be recorded. On the other hand, facsimiles provide readers with access to the original object, directing the reader's attention to the "entirety of the material character of the relevant witnesses."[9] Inasmuch as a digital representation of the witness can, these bibliographic codes—the handwriting, the orthographic peculiarities, the font of the letterhead, the hastily scrawled postscript—aid the reader in making meaning of the work. They serve to place the reader more directly in the moment of reception, allowing the present day reader to narrow the distance between the letter's intended readership and the present.

There is another feature of digital editions that differs profoundly from print editions. That is the method of publication and distribution. Allowing for deterioration or damage, a book remains the same over time. The next time a reader returns to it, it will be in the same font, it will have the same index items referring to the same pagination, table of contents, and text. Electronic publication shifts these expectations. By changing one's browser the display results from the same search may (and typically do) appear different. Electronic repositories tend to be fluid, with content added or changed in ways that are not transparent to the user. Content is migrated to new platforms and data delivery systems; functionality is added, discarded, or changed. Whole sites disappear. While print editions serve as both the storage mechanism for the text, as well as its vehicle of delivery,[10] electronic publication separates the storage from the delivery of texts.

With print publication, the goal of an edition of letters is to present a window onto the lives of the correspondents. Typically edited with a single readership in mind, the editor makes specific choices about the editorial method employed, as well as the level and type of apparatus (notes, introductory material, bibliographical information, etc.). The print publication was the goal of the project. It may be argued, however, that the goals change when editing for electronic publication. It is possible to encode texts with more than one readership in mind, creating in effect two editions in one, providing alternative views of annotation and introductory materials for a secondary school audience and a scholarly audience. What readers engage with in electronic publication is only the surface—the most ephemeral and volatile aspect of the edition. Unlike the book in which readers engage with both surface and medium, electronic editions have many layers. Objects which are operated on computationally represent the text in fluid and dynamic ways. What the system presents to the reader may not be the object stored in the system, but a combination of objects brought together by the database as the result of a reader request.

These items can be recombined and represented to the reader via different views. This is profoundly different from our expectations of print in which we expect stability, consistency—indeed, a kind of permanence. What electronic editions offer is volatility and instability, but it is through these very features that readers are able to engage with texts in performative ways not possible in print.

With these goals, technical considerations, and editorial practices in mind, I and several of my colleagues at University of Maryland Libraries,[11] two outside editorial collaborators (Ann Saddlemyer and Cormac O'Malley), a designer, Eric White, and programmer, Amit Kumar, have been engaged not only in editing two collections of letters for online publication, but creating a new interface and architecture to meet the demands of this document type.

THOMAS MACGREEVY AS CORRESPONDENT

Thomas MacGreevy (1893–1967), Irish modernist poet and art and literary critic, and Director of the National Gallery of Ireland (1950–1963), was an inveterate correspondent, making, keeping, and corresponding with friends throughout his long life. Born in Tarbert County, Kerry in the waning days of the British Empire, MacGreevy joined the British Civil Service, first being posted to Dublin (1910–1912), and then to London (1912–1916). In 1916 he joined the British Army as a second lieutenant with the Royal Field Artillery, returning to Dublin upon demobilization to take up a scholarship for ex-British officers at Trinity College, Dublin. In 1925 he returned to London, and in 1928 moved to Paris. By late 1933 he had returned to London, and in 1941 moved back to Dublin where he remained until his death. Along the way he amassed a collection of personal papers that Trinity College counts as one of its most valued. It documents his rich life in large measure through the many thousands of letters to his friends, associates, and acquaintances. Many of these individuals were some of the most important writers between the wars and include Richard Aldington, Samuel Beckett, Babette Deutsch, T.S. Eliot, James Joyce, Ezra Pound, Lennox Robinson, Edith Somerville, Wallace Stevens, and both the Yeats brothers, Jack and W.B. There are also many correspondences with individuals who were noted in other fields, such as Thomas Bodkin, Jean Coulomb, Harry Clarke, Joan Junyer, Constant Lambert Jean Thomas, or were instrumental in the careers of more famous individuals, such as publishers Charles Putnam, James B. Pinker, Charles Prentice, and A.S. Frere Reeves.

The two correspondences we chose to begin with came about because of a confluence of events: interest in collaborating from individuals outside *The MacGreevy Archive* project team, families and holding repositories willing to grant permission to publish the materials online, and a faculty grant from University of Maryland Libraries. The first correspondence http://www.macgreevy.org/collections/omalley/index.html is between Thomas MacGreevy and Ernie O'Malley. O'Malley (1898–1975) was an officer in the I.R.A. during the Irish War of Independence and Civil War and met MacGreevy briefly while on the run, memorably recounted in his memoirs, *On Another Man's Wound*. He was also a writer, art critic, and art collector. The two men shared an appreciation of contemporary Irish art and were two of the few art critics to champion the work of modernist Irish artists. In the mid-1930s they renewed their friendship, leaving seven extant letters from the late 1930s and 1940s. They capture a foreboding of the impending war, O'Malley's sense of unreality living in a rural part of Ireland during this period, as well as MacGreevy's involvement in the evacuation of the paintings from the National Gallery in London to Wales for safekeeping.

The second collection is much larger in scope. *Thomas MacGreevy and George Yeats: a Friendship in Letters* http://www.macgreevy.org/collections/gyeats/index.html is an edition of correspondence between George Yeats (1893–1968), the English-born wife of the Irish poet W.B. Yeats, herself a formidable critic as well as muse to her husband, and MacGreevy. MacGreevy and Yeats corresponded for forty-one years. Their extant correspondence comprises 148 letters from 1922, shortly after their first meeting in Dublin through 1965, several years before their deaths (MacGreevy in 1967, Yeats in 1968). Miraculously, a majority of both sides of the correspondence has been persevered. The correspondence was at its most intense from 1925 (when MacGreevy moved to London) to 1935. The letters deal with Irish and British culture, art, and writing; with W.B.'s politics and poetry; with family matters and gossip, and news of their wide circle of friends: Lennox Robinson, Ezra

Pound, T.S. Eliot, Richard Aldington, James Joyce and Samuel Beckett, to name but a few.

These correspondences create an alternative narrative of the correspondents' lives, times, and culture, allowing their stories to unfold in a way that no other narrative form allows. Finding ways to give readers access to several views of the text and giving them the ability to choose which aspects of the edition suits their objectives for a particular reading session, was the goal of the editions we undertook.

One of the first challenges we encountered was fitting these new document types into the current architecture of *The Thomas MacGreevy Archive* http://macgreevy.org. Established in 1997, the *Archive* was developed as a thematic research collection centering on the life and work of Thomas MacGreevy. Prior to the correspondence, the collection consisted primarily of articles and books, in the main published by MacGreevy. These are delivered to the user as full text. All the texts on the site are encoded according to the *Text Encoding Initiative Guidelines* http://tei-c.org, a powerful international standard for encoding cultural heritage materials.

When work on the letter collections began, the site architecture supported four collections: a static bibliography of MacGreevy's published writings and writings about MacGreevy, with about two-thirds of the articles (approximately 500 of them) republished in full text format; *Thomas MacGreevy and Jack B. Yeats: An Online Broadsheet,* which explores the personal and professional relationship between the two artists; *Thomas MacGreevy Composing a Poem,* a selection of MacGreevy's poetry presented in multiple versions through the *Versioning Machine* http://v-machine.org, and *Who's Who in the Archive,* an authority database of all the proper names mentioned in the Archive, some 2000 of them.

It became clear at the very early stages of the design process that for the repository to support the letters significant changes would need to be made at all levels: from encoding practice, to display, to system architecture. The majority of these changes were driven by interface needs. These included multiple views of each witness, providing seamless access to biographic information from within the letter interface[12] as many of the people mentioned are unfamiliar to a contemporary audience, annotation, and introductory materials. Except for the facsimile witness and integrated access to biographical notes, the requirements for the collections fit nicely into the paradigm established for "Thomas MacGreevy and Jack B Yeats: An Online Broadsheet".

Like the "Online Broadsheet", each of the collections of correspondence has its own "boutique look". Each has a home page which provides links to an introductory essay, a table of contents (or browse facility), the *MacGreevy Archive* search page, and a credits page. The introduction and credits pages are static. The table of contents, however, for the collections of correspondence are dynamically created each time a user makes a request. This dynamic feature was important to facilitate flexibility in

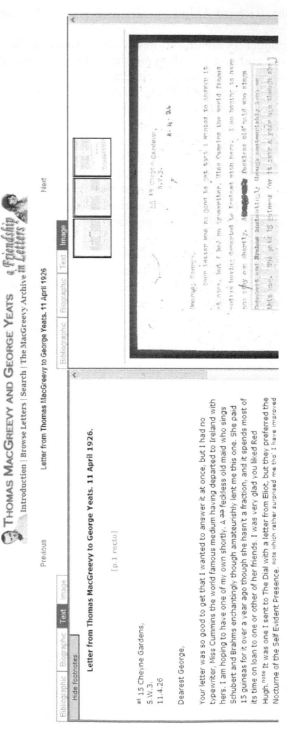

Figure 3.2   The default letter view, with the diplomatic encoded text on the left, and the image view on the right. Permission granted for reprint by A P Watt Ltd on behalf of Gráinne Yeats.

adding new letters to the collection as they come to light as well as to reorder letters already in the system. The default mode for displaying the letters is chronological, but because the index page is dynamically generated the option to present the letters in a different order—by author or by theme, for example—is possible. We could even allow for multiple tabs to provide access to all these views.

Another reason for having the TOC dynamically driven was because of the chunks of data pulled from the TEI/XML encoded text when a reader makes a request of the system. Whereas sufficient semantic information is conveyed by displaying the title of an article as well as the name of the author, a similar display of letters would reveal only the dates of composition and the author (for example, "Letter from Thomas MacGreevy to George Yeats, 26 November 1926"). Unless the searcher had extensive knowledge of the author's and recipient's lives, this information would be insufficient as it gives no insight as to the letter's content. While for material intended for publication, extracting the first 100 characters of a text and displaying it along with the title could be sufficient to give readers semantic clues as to the scope of the text, with correspondence the first 100 characters would convey extremely little. As a remedy, a decision was made to write brief abstracts for each letter and to have them display along with the title, date, author, and keywords in an initial retrieval.

THE CORRESPONDENCE
OF ERNIE O'MALLEY
AND THOMAS MACGREEVY

INTRODUCTION
BROWSE LETTERS
SEARCH
MACGREEVY HOME

Results

Your search yielded 7 letters:

Letter from Ernie O'Malley to Thomas MacGreevy, 6 March 1939
Abstract Invites MacGreevy for the Easter holidays; mentions that MacGreevy had not answered his previous letter; his life at Burrishoole.

Keywords Social Life, Art

Letter from Ernie O'Malley to Thomas MacGreevy, 05 April 1939
Abstract O'Malley writing from Dublin; awaiting letter from MacGreevy; encloses fare so MacGreevy can visit them in Mayo; recounts visit with with Jack Yeats.

Keywords Domestic Life, Social Life

Letter from Ernie O'Malley to Thomas MacGreevy, 01 May 1939
Abstract How O'Malley injured his hand sailing on Easter Sunday; recounts a trip to Dublin where he purchased Jack B Yeats's painting Death for Only One; the Cezanne exhibition in London; suggests that MacGreevy approach his publisher Houghton Mifflin regarding MacGreevy's monograph on Jack Yeats; his translation of Rilke's Letters to a Young Poet; the war in

Figure 3.3 The first results page for the Thomas MacGreevy/Ernie O'Malley correspondence.

While the team agreed on the need for abstracts, their creation went through several permutations. The use of abstracts was tested with the O'Malley collection which proved amenable to abstract writing—the letters were relatively short and contained a limited number of themes. It was possible to encapsulate (using full sentences) the salient points contained in each letter. But when the same approach was used on the Yeats/MacGreevy collection, in which letters could run five to seven pages and cover a multitude of topics, from news, to politics, to the theater, to gossip, the methodology developed was not suitable.

While abstracts are not unheard of in print collections, their role in the online edition is different as it is a means of navigation. In some ways abstracts have the same function as a back of the book index in which the reader engages with surrogates as a means of deciding whether a letter is of interest. The abstracts are one way of compensating for the difficulty of browsing an electronic archive. While it is easy to pick up a book and flip through its pages, stopping to read where one's eye spots an interesting topic or flip back and forth between the index and the text, that ease and serendipity have been difficult to replicate in electronic environments. Abstracts attempt to compensate for the difficulty of browsing through the archive. But an abstract is a surrogate (as are the keywords also displayed on the first results page), and one, necessarily, chooses which information to privilege. In condensing long, rambling, often subtlety-phrased passages into short, terse, grammatically incorrect phrase-level units (the latter in the interest of saving a few words here and there) we might also be misleading readers into deciding that a particular letter is not of interest to them. Other routes into the texts mitigate some of this intervention—for example, a person who is not mentioned in an abstract although she is mentioned in a letter could be found by doing a full text search via the advanced search page.

As mentioned previously, *The MacGreevy Archive* maintains its own name authority, *Who's Who in the MacGreevy Archive*. The authority control was established in 1997 in Microsoft Access as a project management tool. At that time, Library of Congress and Getty Authority files were not publicly available online; moreover, many of the Irish people mentioned are still not well documented in American or British biographical sources. As the project grew out of the Access database, it was converted to XML and made publicly available. This proved to be an advantage in facilitating dynamic linking between database storing the letters and database storing the biographical entries. At first mouseovers were used to indicate that a bio note was present, with an icon indicating its presence. In early versions of the interface, different icons were used to indicate annotation and biographical notes. But as an individual could be mentioned five or ten times in a letter coupled with so many proper names mentioned in each letter, the icon itself became a distraction. We experimented with using different icons, and with having the bio note linked to only the first occurrence of the proper name in each letter, but both proved unsatisfactory.

THOMAS MACGREEVY AND GEORGE YEATS *a Friendship in Letters*

Introduction | Browse Letters | Search | The MacGreevy Archive

Previous Letter from George Yeats to Thomas MacGreevy [December 1923] Next

| Bibliographic | Biographic | Text | Image |

Letter from George Yeats to Thomas MacGreevy. [December 1923].

[p.1]

Cuala Industries
82 Merrion Square
Dublin
Telephone 3298
Embroidery—
{Miss Lily Yeats
{Mrs. W.B. Yeats

Dear Mr McGreevy.

I found a wire from Willy saying I must come over this morning — It is now 1.30 am. — So I just cursed & wrote 19 out of 30 letters & got my books totted up - And tomorrow evening I shall be totting it down the Tottenham Court Road."¹

I wish I could think of an alternative to "Mister McGreevy" but I cant, & "Tom" has the

| Bibliographic | Biographic | Text | Image |

Geoffrey Phibbs
1900 - 1956
writer, editor
⊞ Biographic Note

b Norfolk (later in life changed his surname to Taylor); raised in Sligo, at the family home at Lisheen; educated at Haleybury. He enlisted in the Officer's Training Corps attached to Queen's University, but the Armistice was signed before he saw action Phibbs first began publishing poetry in the early 1920s, and by 1928 had two books published with the Hogarth Press (which were, to a large extent, underwritten by Phibbs). In 1924 he married the painter Norah McGuinness, but the marriage broke up when he entered into a ménage à quatre in 1929 with Robert Graves, Laura Riding, and Graves's wife, Nancy Nicholson (with whom Phibbs later lived when the ménage broke up). Phibbs first met W c 1922 while working as a Carnegie Librarian, and the two had a lively correspondence until Phibbs's abandonment of McGuinness. He died in Dublin.

George Yeats
1892 - 1968
artist, writer
⊞ Biographic Note

Born Bertha Georgie Hyde-Lees in Wrexham. Married WB Yeats in October 1917. In 1919 their first child Anne was born, and in 1921 their son Michael. By the early 1920s George Yeats was active in Cuala Industries and The Dublin Drama League. MacGreevy probably met George Yeats in 1919, and they remained friends until MacGreevy's death in 1967.

Thomas MacGreevy
1893 - 1967
critic, museum director, writer

Figure 3.4 A letter from the MacGreevy/Yeats correspondence with the diplomatic text/biographical notes pane visible, with the first two bio notes expanded. Permission granted for reprint by A P Watt Ltd on behalf of Gráinne Yeats.

At the same time, we were experimenting with how best to display all the information components we felt were necessary for the edition: multiple versions of the text, biographic notes, bibliographic (or TEI header) information, and annotation. We experimented with chunking the data on the screen, and with rollouts, but in the end decided to work with two panes, allowing readers to control which data they wanted to view simultaneously. There have been a number of styling and browser compatibility issues with these panes, yet they give users great flexibility in choosing what information is most important to them and having that information displayed in a readable format on the screen. Now the biographic notes have their own pane and annotation appears as a mouseover from within the text.

It is clear that electronic editions, more so than traditional print editions, are highly constructed, fluid, and interpretative. As Claus Huitfeldt has noted, "there are no facts about a text which are objective in the sense of not being interpretational."[13] Although there is greater transparency in our editorial methods (users can easily compare the diplomatic version of the text to the facsimile) users have access only to the surface of our editions; the decisions we have made in text encoding, in how much information to capture in image creation, in how the indexing functions, is opaque. Moreover, images are still poor surrogates for the originals: they cannot capture the texture of the paper, they may not be able to display watermarks, and because we had to scan images from a microfilm rather than the originals (at the insistence of the holding repositories), letters are reduced to grayscale.

On the other hand, the ease of making changes to online editions makes it trivial for us to re-date letters, correct annotation, or revise incorrect transcription as this information comes to light. Full-text searching provides users with unprecedented access to the texts in ways not possible in print publication. Although much of the goal of electronic editing has been to emulate, in some fashion, print, it is through the as yet unrealized possibilities of deformative procedures we enact on the text that patterns and relationships that may not be evident in codex presentations, or indeed, when engaging with the original objects are revealed, ultimately forcing us to see, as Jerome McGann has written in *Radiant Textuality*, what we don't know that we know.[14]

Because the letters are encoded according to a schema as rich as the TEI in which it is possible to isolate blocks or types of text (all annotation, for example, or all titles of works of art) the edition will be well positioned to take advantage of the current research in data mining and visualization. Currently the pages that are returned to the reader owe much to the linearity of print culture. Other options might be to cluster search results or display them in graphs giving readers the tools to work with the text outside a narrative space.

As Buzetti and McGann have written, "[s]cholarly editions are a special, highly sophisticated type of self-reflexive communication": one that can "transform social and documentary aspects of the book into computable code."[15] We are still at early days of understanding the possibilities of creating critical editions as collaborative and dynamic work spaces, not just for editors, but for readers: a machine that organizes and performs computation on data (linguistic, moving or still images, or sound) for complex study and analysis. That these objects are brought into synthetic relation to one another, that they may be manipulated and displayed in a variety of visualizations is the real strength of the electronic critical edition. Being able to manipulate entire texts, chunks of texts or semantic units as objects which can be recombined are the building blocks for recreation and reconstruction that will create new visual palettes prompting questions to be asked of the data that the original correspondents, the latter day editors, and the designers of the system never imagined.

NOTES

1. Phill Berrie et al, "Authenticating Electronic Editions," in *Electronic Textual Editing*, ed. Lou Burnard, Katherine O'Brien O'Keeffe, John Unsworth (New York: Modern Language Association, 2006), 270.
2. Ralph A Leigh, "Rousseau's Correspondence; Editorial Problems," in *Editing Correspondence: Papers given at the Fourteenth Annual Conference on Editorial Problems,* ed. J.A. Dainard (New York: Garland Publishing, 1979), 39–62.
3. Hester Piozzi, *Letters To and From the Late Samuel Johnson, LL.D., To Which Are Added, Some Poems Never Before Printed* (London: Strahan, 1788), ii.
4. Piozzi, iii.
5. John H Middendorf, "Eighteenth-Century English Literature," in *Scholarly Editing: a Guide to Research*, ed. D.C. Greetham (New York: Modern Language Association, 1995), 288.
6. Piozzi, v.
7. F. Richard J. Cox, "Messrs. Washington, Jefferson, and Gates: Quarelling about the Preservation of the Documentary Heritage of the United States," *First Monday* 2: 8 http://www.firstmonday.org/issues/issue2_8/cox/index.html. August 1997.
8. Paul Eggert, "Text-encoding, Theories of the Text, and the 'Work-Site," *Literary and Linguistic Computing*, 20, no. 4 (2005): 428.
9. Dino Buzzetti and Jerome McGann, "Critical Editing in a Digital Horizon" in *Electronic Textual Editing*, eds. Lou Burnard, Katharine O'Brien O'Keeffe, John Unsworth (New York: Modern Language Association, 2006), 57.
10. Espen J. Aarseth, *Cybertext: Perspectives on Ergodic Literature* (Baltimore: Johns Hopkins Press, 1997), 10–11.
11. My thanks to my colleagues at University of Maryland, Sean Daugherty, Aiden Faust, Gretchen Gueguen, and Jennifer Roper.
12. Without this feature, users would have had to toggle between two separate interfaces—one that showed the letters, and one that was being generated directly from the MacGreevy Names Database.
13. Claus Huitfeldt, "Multi-dimensional Texts in a One-Dimensional Medium,"*Computers and the Humanities* 28, nos. 4–5 (July 1994): 23.
14. Jerome McGann, *Radiant Textuality: Literature After the World Wide Web* (New York: Palgrave, 2001), 207.
15. Buzetti and McGann, 69.

4   The Harvard Project on the Soviet Social System Online

Margaret E. Hale, Richard Lesage, and Bradley L. Schaffner

At the end of the Second World War, between 250,000 and 500,000 Soviet citizens found themselves living outside of the borders of the USSR in Western Europe, the United States, and beyond.[1] For approximately six years after the cessation of hostilities, many of these individuals lived in displaced person camps. This high concentration of dislocated citizens provided Western scholars with a unique opportunity to study Soviet society first-hand by interviewing these émigrés concerning their lives under communist rule. Of course, such access to rank and file citizens living in the Soviet Union was not possible, given the closed and totalitarian nature of the Soviet government and society. Indeed, intelligence agencies from many Allied powers took advantage of this opportunity to interview some émigrés in an effort to better understand the Soviet Union. However, these interactions targeted specific people, particularly those who held positions of responsibility in the military and/or government, rather than attempting to analyze the general population. By the early 1950s, the displaced person camps were shutting down as Soviet and other refugees relocated across Europe and beyond, making it more difficult to identify, locate, and interview these people. The final closure of the camps could potentially signal that a unique opportunity to learn about the everyday lives of Soviet citizens had slipped away.

Fortunately, at the end of the 1940s, scholars at Harvard University's Russian Research Center (RRC), now known as the Davis Center for Russian and Eurasian Studies, realized that the exiled Soviet community concentrated in Western Europe represented a once-in-a-career opportunity to study the USSR based on that country's own citizens' observations and thoughts, rather than through the educated speculations of scholars observing from abroad. These researchers put in motion a plan to gather data from these displaced persons in an effort to collect unique information on the political, economic, social, and cultural conditions of the Soviet Union.

In the summer of 1949, senior RRC scholars conducted a series of test interviews with a small group of Soviet refugees that "established the feasibility and value of a large-scale interviewing project."[2] In early 1950, as a result of this successful pilot project, the Russian Research Center obtained funding from the Human Resources Institute, an Air Force intelligence agency located at Maxwell Air Force Base in Alabama, to carry out a full-scale interview project.[3] The resulting program became known as the *Harvard Project on the Soviet System (HPSSS)*, also referred to as the *Harvard Refugee Project*.

The interviews and data gathering took place between 1950 and 1951 (with a few interviews taking place as late as 1953). The primary émigré community surveyed, centered in western Germany, caused the RRC staff to work in coordination with the Institute for the Study of the USSR located in Munich. A few interviews also were conducted in Austria. Finally, a smaller exile community located in the United States also was interviewed as part of a control group. The data acquired through 764 interviews, 60 psychological tests, and 12,466 questionnaires attempted to provide an overview and understanding of day-to-day life in the Soviet Union from 1917 through the late 1940s.[4]

The interviews conducted in Russian, Ukrainian, or other languages of the Soviet Union, were transcribed in English and reproduced by ditto-master for analysis and preservation.[5] The interview data was divided into two sets, "Series A" and "Series B." The former (also referred to as Schedule A) dealt with personal history, covering the interviewee's "work and educational history, his family background and relations, his sources of information—reading and listening habits and attitudes towards them—his social and political attitudes and a history of his relations to the regime."[6] "Series B" (also referred to as Schedule B) supplemented this information and focused on specialized knowledge, such as the operation of Soviet factories, the medical system, the training of lawyers, problems of national minorities, and life under German occupation.[7] "Series A" interviews consist of thirty-seven volumes, and "Series B" of twenty-four, with basic indexing completed separately.[8] These sixty-one volumes, along with the corresponding files, indexes, and guides were then deposited in the Harvard University library system.

It is beyond the scope of this article to discuss the actual project or the resulting findings and publications in depth. However, two of the earliest monographs resulting from the research, *How the Soviet System Works*[9] and *The Soviet Citizen: Daily Life in a Totalitarian Society*[10] served as published final reports of the undertaking and provide detailed overviews of the research conducted, including methodologies and criticisms leveled against the endeavor.[11]

The value of this venture is witnessed through the number of publications that utilized the data and information acquired. Within eight years of the enterprise's completion, (1952–1960) at least fifty-three books and articles were published utilizing the *HPSSS*.[12] Since that time, far fewer studies have been published based on this investigation. Part of the reason for the decrease in the use of this research can be explained by the fact that the information had become dated, but this does not fully account for the decline in publications. One must also consider that much of the raw data simply is not easily accessible. The materials are poorly indexed, making them challenging to use.[13] In addition, the physical condition of the copies of the ditto-masters continues to deteriorate, making many pages in the bound volumes difficult to read. Finally, the materials must be used in the libraries that house them, many of which are not open to the general public.

While use of the data and related information has declined since the 1960s, the value of this collection as a research and teaching tool remains high. The challenges of using these data sets aside, a number of professors at Harvard University have utilized the *HPSSS* as a primary resource for both undergraduate and graduate student research projects.

Given the complex organization of the study, combined with the increasingly fragile nature of the materials, the *HPSSS* was identified as a likely candidate for digitization by two professors, Dr. Terry Martin, Department of History at Harvard University and Dr. David Brandenberger, Department of History, University of Richmond in Virginia, and a Harvard graduate, who responded to a call put out by the Harvard University Library (HUL) for proposals for the creation of digital research projects that would have an immediate and demonstrable use to Harvard's academic community for teaching and research. This grant program was called the "Library Digital Initiative" or LDI for short.[14]

The LDI competitive process grant program invited teaching faculty and librarians from across the university to submit proposals for the creation of digital resources. For seven years, from 1999 through 2006, HUL provided money to fund ten rounds of awards, during which thirty-nine projects received funds and were completed.[15]

The origins of the *HPSSS Online* digital resource, like many of the other projects created with LDI funds, was distinctive in that teaching faculty approached the library with the idea for the project, rather than librarians developing it and then searching for faculty who would support the undertaking, as so often happens with this type of venture. Teaching faculty at both Harvard and the University of Richmond drafted the initial proposal as a way to support their pedagogical endeavors, particularly with undergraduates. They then worked with librarians of the Slavic Division of the Harvard College Library and of the Davis Center for Russian and Eurasian Studies to fully conceptualize the project for the grant proposal.

Dr. Brandenberger writes in the LDI proposal that the *HPSSS* research includes:

> extensive one-of-a-kind data on political, economic, social and cultural conditions of the USSR during this period. The study's value is enhanced by the fact that it was compiled in English and organized according to a rigorous social science framework making it accessible to a broad range of students and scholars beyond those fluent in Russian.

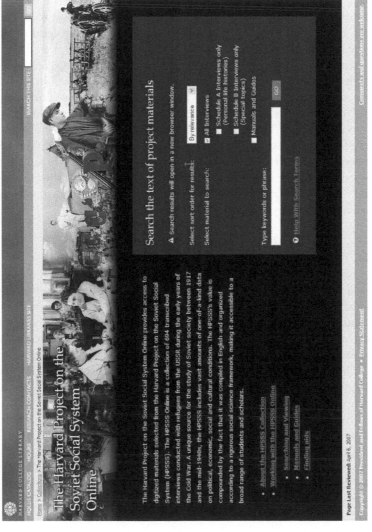

Figure 4.1 The HPSSS Online Web Site.

Ultimately, the breadth, depth and English-language accessibility of the *HPSSS* provide it with enormous potential, both as a teaching tool in the classroom and within a wider community of scholars on Soviet history, literature and cultural studies.[16]

The review committee found these arguments persuasive and granted funds to digitize much of the *HPSSS* through LDI in 2005. The *Harvard Project on the Soviet Social System Online* was completed in the spring of 2007 and may now be accessed on the Web at http://nrs.harvard.edu/urn-3:hul.eresource:hpsoviet.

The staff of the Harvard College Library Imaging Services developed and carried out the actual digitization project. They worked in close coordination with the teaching faculty and librarians involved in the grant proposal to successfully complete the digitization project in a little over twelve months time. The nature and condition of the materials found in the sixty-four volumes of "Series A" and "Series B" presented many unique challenges and as a result, both established procedures as well as some new approaches were utilized by Imaging Services to deal with this unique material. The focus of this chapter is to provide an overview of how the Harvard staff completed this project.

PROJECT IMPLEMENTATION

The project involved the digitization of the transcriptions of interviews conducted with refugees from the USSR in the early 1950s, as well as various manuals and guides to the collection. The project goal was to link fully searchable versions of each *HPSSS* interview to an electronic finding aid; additionally, the ability to perform a search across all interviews and manuals and guides was needed. Each digitized transcript is comprised of color page images, text for searching and display, and a METS-formatted XML file to facilitate navigation and delivery.

Harvard staff managed the project, created the finding aid and catalog record for discovery, developed a Web site to accommodate searching across interviews, scanned the printed transcripts, assembled all digital components (page images, text files, and METS XML files), and deposited "masters" to the Harvard University Library Digital Repository Service, from which delivery versions are served via Harvard's Page Delivery Service.

REFORMATTING

Prior to the digitization of the *HPSSS* materials, existing copies were reviewed to determine the condition and number of pages and to identify the appropriate sources for digitization. Two paper copies existed of

Schedule A: a bound copy at the Davis Center Library and a disbound copy at the Harvard Depository, the university library system's remote storage facility. The only paper copy available of Schedule B was a disbound copy at the Harvard Depository. Although both Schedules A and B had been microfilmed, Imaging Services staff determined that the poor quality of the original materials (the interviews consist of mimeographed pages with a purple type where the text is often unclear or the print has faded) resulted in microfilm images of inferior quality that could not be scanned for digital conversion. The disbound copies of Schedule A and B, totaling approximately 26,300 pages, were identified as the best source for digitization. Only one copy was available for the approximately 1,500 pages of supplementary materials (manuals and guides).

Two workflows were established for digitization: a studio camera workflow and a sheet fed workflow. For materials for which only one copy existed (Schedule B and the manuals and guides) digitization was done utilizing a studio camera. For materials with duplicate copies, approximately 18,500 pages, project staff used a document scanner equipped with a sheet feeder. TIFF images were created as master copies, with lossy compressed JPEG2000 images for delivery. In the lossy compression method of compressing data and then decompressing it, the data that is retrieved may be different from the original, but is close enough to be of use.

All materials were collated by the Project Archivist prior to digitization. During this preparation process, the Archivist recorded descriptive data for each interview for later use in labeling the digital objects and in the creation of a finding aid.

TEXT CONVERSION

Early in this endeavor, faculty advisors indicated that the ability to search the full text of each interview would be of tremendous value to the scholarly community. Therefore, project staff explored keyword searching of the text as the primary means of access to the content of the interviews. Unfortunately, due to the poor quality of the original copies, initial tests of Optical Character Recognition (OCR) software on the page images proved unsatisfactory and the staff determined that re-keying or OCR correction would be needed to successfully meet the goal of producing a searchable resource. Ultimately, re-keying was utilized.

It is important to note that the re-keying of the interviews did not eliminate the need for direct capture of the source materials. David Brandenberger, Project Associate, provided the following reasons for making images of the original transcripts available:

1) the *HPSSS* interview transcripts are "working copies" rather than standardized, edited and polished book chapters. As such,

they have important idiosyncrasies (spelling irregularities, foreign words, purple prose, struck-out text) that a historian can tease meaning from. For example, what may seem like awkward wording or syntax to a non-specialist may to a historian be evidence of the literal translation of an obscure Russian expression or proverb. Transcription of this material into a text file would make these idiosyncrasies harder to spot and generally make the entire document look more formal, polished and standardized than it really is.

2) transcription of the interviews into a more formal and polished framework would reduce their usefulness as an archival document in the classroom. Many undergraduates have never had exposure to the raw and unpolished world of archival documentation; the *HPSSS* Online project offers a chance to challenge such students with something other than standardized, perfectly legible fonts and formatted pages that they are familiar with from textbooks and online newspapers. Put another way, the *HPSSS Online* project allows the historian the opportunity to emphasize to students that reading an archival document is not necessarily the same as reading a printed page.

3) transcription risks introducing distortions into the text as data entry technicians accidentally "correct" misspellings, add missing words or fix "incorrect" syntax in the interviews. Having the image of the original document available would allow students and researchers to quote the *HPSSS* interviews with total confidence that they are quoting from the original source itself.

4) transcription would likely eliminate the hand-drawn figures, charts and diagrams currently present in some of the interviews.

For the first time, Imaging Services pursued the use of an outside vendor for text conversion services. Project staff developed a Request for Information (RFI) and sent it to three vendors. The RFI identified qualified companies that could provide preliminary pricing for the transcription—via keying, or via OCR with correction—of machine-printed English text to ASCII files (txt format). The ASCII text was to be at the page level, preserving the word order of the originals. Staff expected that the level of accuracy mandated for the ASCII quality would depend on pricing and vendors were asked to indicate price differences at the typical unit(s) (e.g., character, word, and page) and typical accuracy thresholds. Other than joining an end-of-line hyphenated word into a single word in the transcribed file, no text processing or markup was required.

A Request for Proposal to two vendors followed the RFI in which HCL Imaging Services sought to outsource two production tasks to a capable service bureau:

- creation of highly accurate transcriptions from source digital page images, and;
- production of tab-delimited files that associate page numbers with file names.

Imaging Services selected Data Conversion Laboratory, Inc. (DCL) based on the quality of samples, cost, and positive reviews from another Harvard project utilizing this vendor. Due to the quality of the input files, DCL could not guarantee a specific level of accuracy, but committed to making a best effort to record the data precisely. They projected accuracy levels similar to those in the samples provided. Given the quality of the sample and the acknowledgement that the quality of the page images did not lend itself to a predictable accuracy rates, Imaging Services found this agreement acceptable.

Imaging Services established a workflow in which JPEG images of the pages were sent to the vendor on CD-ROM and text files were returned via FTP in specified directory structure corresponding with the page images. Upon receipt, the text files underwent a quality control review. Following QC, with some minor correction of keywords appearing in the text, files were made available to the programmer in Imaging Services, where a METS file was created, and a deposit package, including METS files, pages images and text files, was deposited into Harvard's Digital Repository Service.

DISCOVERY, ACCESS AND STORAGE

LDI funded projects are expected to make use of Harvard's Digital Library infrastructure developed though the Library Digital Initiative. The infrastructure includes systems for Storage and Access Management, Delivery, and Discovery.

Project staff created a finding aid to the digitized *HPSSS* materials and made it available through OASIS, Harvard's union catalog of finding aids.[17] The finding aid provides contextual information on the materials as well as a list of all Schedule A and Schedule B interviews, and the various digitized manuals and guides. Links are provided to the digital version of each interview, delivered through the Page Delivery Service (PDS), Harvard's page turning service for delivering multi-page documents to Web browsers.[18]

Each interview, manual or guide is a unique digital object delivered through the PDS. Descriptive label information for the digital object is displayed in the PDS. The PDS allows a user to page through the digital object or to go to a specific page. The option of a printable version is provided, allowing for a PDF of the digital object to be created on the fly for downloading or printing. Users can choose to view the page image or the keyed full text behind the page image. The PDS also allows for the

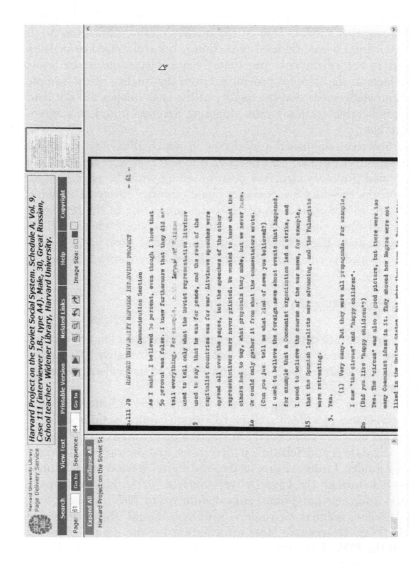

Figure 4.2   A document in the PDS.

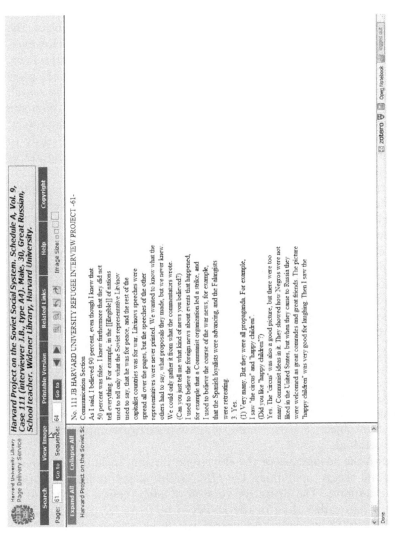

Figure 4.3   Keyed full text behind the page image.

viewing of the page image in various sizes and for zooming in on specific parts of the image.

Within the PDS it is also possible to search the keyed full text of the page turned object by using the Full Text Search Service (FTS), another component of Harvard's digital library infrastructure.[19] The FTS provides a mechanism for the indexing and retrieval of textual digital objects. Search options include Boolean operators, quoted phrases and proximity.

By making each interview, manual or guide a single digital object, the ability to search the individual document using FTS is possible. However, the ability to search across a series of interviews or across all interviews, manuals and guides was also desired. To accommodate this need, project staff developed a Web site that provides an FTS search form to search multiple digital objects. In addition to the search interface, the Web site provides contextual information, background on the history of the project, and assistance with searching and using the collection. Links directly to manuals and guides are provided, as well as a link to the finding aid in OASIS to allow users to browse the list of interviews.

Links to the newly developed resource were added to existing bibliographic records for Schedules A and B in HOLLIS, Harvard's Web-based public bibliographic catalog. A librarian also created a record in HOLLIS for the newly developed online resource, with a link to the resource as well as to the electronic finding aid in OASIS, and registered the Web site as a Harvard digital resource so that the research tool can be found in the electronic resources section of Harvard's Library Portal.[20]

Page images and accompanying text and metadata files are stored in Harvard's Digital Repository Service (DRS).[21] The DRS provides Harvard affiliated owners of digital material with a storage and retrieval system for their collections. Digital Repository services and facilities include an electronic storage facility within which the digital objects created or purchased by Harvard agencies reside; management of administrative and structural metadata associated with stored objects; preservation policies and procedures to ensure the continued usability of stored objects; and delivery of an object to a registered or known software application (e.g., an online catalog).

Even with the advantages of the electronic version, including enhanced searching and access capabilities, the *HPSSS Online* still reflects the original, paper resource. The definitive version of each interview is found in the page images rather than in the re-keyed text. As Dr. Brandenberger noted, "the *HPSSS* interview transcripts are 'working copies' rather than standardized, edited and polished book chapters. As such, they have idiosyncrasies . . ." Indeed, both the users of the original version as well as the electronic version will encounter special challenges because of the way that the interviews were conducted and transcribed. The interviews were conducted in the subject's native language (Russian or Ukrainian for example). At the conclusion of the session, the interviewer would translate his notes into English. As a result, program staff had very little time to work on these translations and therefore, there are often literal translations that one would not normally find in more polished versions of such text. For example, the Soviet film entitled *Veselye rebiata* is translated as *Happy Children*, when the actual title is *Happy / Happy-go-lucky Guys*, with rebiata referring to "guys" rather than children. In Russian, "happy children" would be "veselye deti."

Although *HPSSS Online* has only been publicly accessible for less than three months (over the summer), it has already been selected to serve as the central resource for a Harvard undergraduate history research seminar. The professor is utilizing *HPSSS Online* both because of its content and due to the fact that it will provide undergraduate students with the opportunity to conduct original research using archival documents. It is likely that had this resource not been digitized, the professor would not have chosen the paper version of the *HPSSS* for the course given its complex nature and its inaccessibility.

The LDI program selected The *Harvard Project on the Soviet Social System* for digitization because it is a resource that has both a scholarly and pedagogical value. Although the information gathered is dated, it still has great research value and the *HPSSS* continues to be utilized by scholars, both Russian/Soviet experts, and by those who can not read Russian. *HPSSS Online* now provides these researchers with the opportunity to utilize this resource through their computer. Because the texts of the interviews are now fully searchable, project administrators expect researchers will find even more ways to analyze the data acquired.

While the *HPSSS* has been regularly consulted by researchers, its use in the classroom has been more limited. This is a result of the complex nature of using the sixty-one volumes of interviews and the indexes and guides. Simply stated, the paper and microfilm versions are difficult to use. Students could spend a whole semester or more attempting to identify relevant information. The *HPSSS Online* now provides straightforward online searching allowing a student to identify topics of interest quickly and easily. In addition, because the resource is built around the page images of the original documents, students have the opportunity to learn to work with archival material, including learning how to deal with the quirks of using such resources.

NOTES

1. Alex Inkeles and Raymond A. Bauer, *The Soviet Citizen: Daily Life in a Totalitarian Society* (Cambridge, MA: Harvard University Press, 1959), 5.
2. Inkeles and Bauer, 9.
3. Contract AF No. 33 (038)-12909.
4. Raymond A. Bauer, Alex Inkeles, and Clyde Kluckhohn, *How the Soviet System Works: Cultural, Psychological & Social Themes* (New York: Vintage

Books, 1960), 8–10. Copies of the written questionnaires can be found in Inkeles and Bauer, *The Soviet Citizen*, 401–430.

5. The 12,466 questionnaires were tabulated and discarded.
6. Bauer, Inkeles, and Kluckhohn, 9.
7. Ibid. Marjorie Mandelstam Balzer, who wrote the guide *Materials for the Project on the Soviet Social System*, notes that the Schedule A interviews are "sociological" and the Schedule B interviews are "anthropological." See: Marjorie Mandelstam Balzer, Materials for the Project on the Soviet Social System (Soviet Refugee Interview and Questionnaire Data, 1950–1953, for Air Force Contract No. 33[03])-12909) (Cambridge, MA: Russian Research Center, 1980), p. 2. This guide may be accessed at http://nrs.harvard.edu/urn-3:FHCL:1115531.
8. See Balzer for a complete description of the collection.
9. Bauer, Inkeles, Kluchhohn.
10. Inkeles and Bauer.
11. David Brandenberger, who took the lead in developing the HPSS Online grant proposal and subsequent project, is currently writing a background guide to using the HPSSS Online, which will provide an excellent overview of the project. When finished, this guide should also be available online with the actual resource.
12. Inkeles and Bauer, 464–467.
13. Margorie Mandelstam Balzer's brief guide entitled *Materials for the Project on the Soviet Social System* aptly illustrates how complicated it is to access the paper files and the data generated through this research. See: Marjorie Mandelstam Balzer, *Materials for the Project on the Soviet Social System (Soviet Refugee Interview and Questionnaire Data, 1950–1953, for Air Force Contract No. 33[03])-12909)* (Cambridge, MA: Russian Research Center, 1980). This guide may be accessed at http://nrs.harvard.edu/urn-3:FHCL:1115531.
14. The LDI Program Proposal may be accessed at http://hul.harvard.edu/ldi/html/ldi_origins.html. .
15. See http://hul.harvard.edu/ldi/html/funded_projects.html for a complete list of projects.
16. Harvard University Library, Library Digital Initiative, Round 8, *Harvard Project on the Soviet Social System Online*, July 22, 2005. Unpublished, 2.
17. OASIS can be accessed at http://oasis.harvard.edu/.
18. "The Page Delivery Service (PDS) delivers to a Web browser scanned page images of books, diaries, reports, journals and other multi-page documents from the collections of the Harvard libraries." From "Page Delivery Service: Overview" available at http://hul.harvard.edu/ois/systems/pds. This document provides an overview of the system.
19. More information on the FTS can be found at http://hul.harvard.edu/ois/systems/#fts.
20. See http://eresearch.lib.harvard.edu/V.
21. More information on the DRS can be found at http://hul.harvard.edu/ois/systems/drs/.

5 The Hemeroteca Digital of the National Library of Spain

Elena García-Puente and Lola Rodríguez

INTRODUCTION

In this article, we will present a general overview of the newspaper digitization project that has been carried out at the National Library of Spain over the last ten years. In this overview we will address the two major initiatives undertaken by the National Library concerning the management of serial publications, namely microfilming and digitization, which are particularly focused on newspaper collections. We will first discuss the microfilming project, which began in 1991 and is still under way. Then we will provide the rationale for the digitization project, briefly describe the technical process of digitization, and present the outcomes of this project in terms of the two applications that have been made available to users. Finally, we will comment on the benefits of these projects for users and will outline developments for the near future.

FROM MICROFILMING TO DIGITIZATION

The National Library of Spain has an outstanding collection of Spanish serial publications covering more than 135,000 titles. They date from 1660 to the present and are in a variety of physical conditions. The Press Collection, for example, has been extensively used, and stands to disappear entirely if not preserved. This impending danger led to the adoption of preservation policies for serial publications. These policies focused on contents conservation by means of transfer to other media, which allowed for the removal of paper volumes from the Serials Reading Room. The first initiative was the newspaper microfilming program, which began in 1991. Since then, almost all the titles have been microfilmed up to 1998, including many periodicals. We use silver halide thirty-five millimeter film and conform to all the related ISO standards. Some figures of this program, still in progress, are given below:

- Microfilmed titles: 1,992
- Volumes: 75,622

- Frames: 31,978,026
- Microfilm reels: 55,236
- Microfiches: 7,213

CURRENT NEWSPAPER DIGITIZATION PROJECT

Early attempts related to press digitization began in 1997, when the National Library first microfilmed 187 titles from the nineteenth century, and then digitized these microforms. The outcome of this experiment was quite unsatisfactory: images had black frames, the paper format was damaged and yellowed (which was a problem when OCR was later applied), the illustrations of the publications, photographs and print were not clear enough, the color was faded, and large formats that contained small letters were of poor quality. In spite of that, we were able to recover a large amount of these images, and have digitized again the images that were impossible to read.

The Microfilm Program offered an initial solution in 1998 for consulting our press backfiles, but it was necessary to find a procedure for the consultation of the current titles, which were located at remote storage facilities in Alcalá de Henares, a city located thirty kilometers away from Madrid in Recoletos.

At the same time, the first commercial digitization projects were being launched in Spain. The first was the *Archivo histórico de ABC*, a Spanish newspaper which had been in publication since 1903. The publisher digitized the paper's complete backfile and published a CD-ROM edition. It was then that the National Library started to consider digitization as the solution for consulting current titles.

Accordingly, the Current Newspaper Digitization Program was started in 1999. Because newspapers were microfilmed up to 1998, it was decided that digitization would begin from 1999 onwards. Agreements also were made with newspaper publishers who were digitizing their collections to acquire an electronic copy for the National Library for research purposes. Needless to say, those newspapers with digital versions were excluded from the digitization program.

GOALS OF THE CURRENT NEWSPAPER DIGITIZATION PROJECT

Although the merits of microfilming vs. digitizing have been hotly debated on many occasions, the National Library did not consider digitization as an alternative to microfilming, but as a parallel and complementary process.

The major aim of this project was not long-term preservation. Our main concern was to provide a means of consulting the current collections. Digitization provided an appropriate way to avoid moving a huge amount of volumes located off-site and to offer better access to their contents than microfilm. Therefore, in 1999 the National Library started digitizing 108 newspaper titles from legal deposit. The selection was made according to three parameters:

- exhaustiveness, i.e., trying to cover all titles which were then being published,
- representativeness, i.e., selecting titles from all the Spanish Autonomous Communities, at least one title from each,
- use, i.e., giving priority to the most consulted titles, which were determined according to statistics.

The list of titles selected for digitizing is revised every year, because it is inevitable that changes have to be made. Although the National Library's policy is to continue digitizing the same titles, some of these have to be withdrawn for various reasons: the publication has ceased, it has been digitized by the publisher, or because it is irregularly delivered to the National Library.

Standards

Standards used have varied and evolved over time along with technical improvements. From the beginning, it was agreed that technical specifications should conform to library standards, both to facilitate the exchange of images with other institutions and to make those images more lasting. Therefore, recommendations from UNESCO's "Memory of the World" Program for press digitization were followed: 300 ppp minimal resolution, 1 bit per pixel, images in TIFF file format, with CCITT Group IV compression to white and black and TIFF compression JPEG to grey scale or color. Experts in the field were consulted to select the most appropriate criteria for the project. Since 2004, all the images have been digitized using OCR. In 2006, after an evaluation of tool use, the National Library decided to apply OCR to all previously digitized images. The results are PDF files with hidden text. In addition, all PDF files have thumbnails.

Information Storage

Images resulting from the digitization of current newspapers are stored on CD-ROMs. Two copies are maintained, one being the master or archival copy, which can be migrated to any other format for assuring its permanence. This master is stored in off-site stacks of the National Library in Alcalá de Henares. On an ongoing basis, images are migrated to formats with more capacity, such as DVDs, in order to refresh the information and because of space issues.

HEMEROTECA DIGITAL (DIGITAL NEWSPAPER LIBRARY)

Press digitization at the National Library was a resounding success and was welcomed by users, who appreciated the ease of access it provided in stark contrast to viewing microform reels. In 2006 the Library decided not only to continue the current press project, accessible only within the institution's building, but also to start digitizing historical newspapers and periodicals as well. The result was the digitization of a wide selection of serial titles, and, as a byproduct, the Hemeroteca Digital. This digital library displays 143 titles published between 1772 and 1933 and contains half a million digitized pages. The titles included are copyright free, thus allowing their dissemination on the Internet. They cover a wide variety of subjects, among them:

- Political newspapers, such as *La Iberia*, an outstanding example of a liberal newspaper;
- The satirical press, a genre quite widespread in the nineteenth century, of which *La Flaca* is a remarkable example;
- Literary and artistic journals, such as *El Artista*, and their valuable lithographs;
- Entertainment journals, such as the beautifully illustrated *El Correo de las damas* and *Album Salón*, whose audiences were mostly women;
- Magazines, such as *El Arte del teatro* or *La Lidia*, devoted to theatre and other spectator events, like sports or bullfighting;
- Scientific and technical journals, which provide an overview of the state of the art of science in Spain during these years.

Among the titles, we can find quaint examples that look somewhat funny today, such as *Sicalíptico*, an erotic magazine from the turn of the twentieth century, or *Café*, one of the first free newspapers distributed in Madrid's cafes.

One of the main problems the Serials Department of the National Library of Spain has to deal with is the poor condition of our collection, which is due to several factors:

- Paper acidification: since the last third of the nineteenth century, Spanish paper has been manufactured basically from wood pulp, which severely affects its stability;
- Poor ink and paper quality: newspapers have to be quickly written, typeset and printed. The interest is in the news, not the medium, and therefore these newspapers are usually of very poor quality. They become yellow and brittle after a short period of time, even when preservation policies are adopted;
- Formats: since the nineteenth century, newspapers have used a large size that makes them difficult to handle. They were often folded in

order to fit them onto the shelves, which quite often has badly damaged the copies;

- Bindings: Over the years, binding has been considered the most convenient, protective measure for periodicals collections. Binding prevented the loss of single issues and titles had a physical container to make them stand upright and protect them from dust, light and other environmental factors. However, this has caused many problems as well, such as the cutting of margins, loss of text in the inner part of the volume or misarranged numbers, and also has hampered later processes that may apply to the copy, such as microfilming;

- Integrity: the most important source for the acquisition of newspapers in the National Library is legal deposit, which obliges printers to give the Library a certain amount of copies of every work that is printed in Spain (the number depends on the type of material). Although legal deposit has worked quite well since 1958, when the law was passed, serials and especially issues of daily newspapers have become easier to lose. In the case of newspapers, publishers and printers often assume that different editions can bear the same legal deposit number, which causes trouble in the identification of editions and the gathering of copies, thus creating incomplete runs;

- Use: some serial titles, and especially some newspapers, are very often read or searched at the libraries, and until microform surrogates were filmed there was no format available other than paper. Neither were there many newspaper collections in Spain, since most public libraries did not keep their old newspapers because of lack of space, or because collections had disappeared due to several factors: flooding, fires, etc. As a consequence, the collections of the Hemeroteca Nacional (the Newspaper Library, which became part of the National Library of Spain in 1997) were very heavily used, photocopied and damaged. In addition to this, another important factor that has led to the deterioration of the collection is the mishandling of collections by the library staff over time.

Selection

Since the National Library of Spain keeps more than 135,000 titles of serial publications, a selection of titles is inevitable. Our major aim is to digitize the most relevant titles in order to facilitate their access as quickly as possible. Consequently, due to funding limitations, we have had to establish certain priorities. The main factors are:

- Interest in the work, both for itself and its context;
- Number of consultations of the title, determined by statistical data collected over time;
- Number of copies available, prioritizing those titles that are unique;

- Integrity of the copy, trying to offer the most complete ones;
- Physical condition, digitizing original copies in poor condition in order to withdraw them from public use;
- Representativeness, trying to provide a sample of Spanish culture from all Spanish-speaking colonies and countries during the past centuries.

The importance of the press as a historic tool and primary research resource is widely known. Newspapers offer a vivid and colorful picture of the time when they were launched. They describe the political, social and cultural events of the moment. Advertisements and short notices provide an even more detailed picture of the way of life and of local events. Newspapers also include a lot of information about individuals (births, marriages, professional careers, etc.) which is very useful for researchers, not only for biographical purposes. Unfortunately, this kind of research has been always very cumbersome. There are few indexes to facilitate the search, references are often vague, paper volumes are not easy to locate or browse, runs are incomplete due to missing or cut out numbers, and microfilm reels are hard to deal with. The Internet has dramatically changed this state of affairs by improving access, and now users can obtain information virtually without moving from their chairs. Hemeroteca Digital aims at simplifying the tasks associated with press research in Spain. For researchers, the new digital library may be seen as a tapestry, with lots of different threads woven together that can be separately followed to obtain a variety of perspectives on a given subject.

Hemeroteca Digital is the starting point of the "Biblioteca Digital Hispánica" (in English, the Hispanic Digital Library) project, which aims at promoting the use and public dissemination of the Spanish bibliographic heritage kept at the National Library. Although currently the oldest title dates back to 1772, the scope of the Hemeroteca Digital will range from the seventeenth century to 1933. This upper limit was established in order to allow for the eighty-year period that Spanish regulations require before a work is put in the public domain.

Goals of Hemeroteca Digital

There are three main goals of the Hemeroteca Digital:

- To offer public access to the Spanish National Library collection of old newspapers;
- To become the benchmark for research on the Spanish press;
- To open cooperation channels with other institutions with the aim of locating and completing press collections.

Hemeroteca Digital started out with the main objective of becoming the central site for Spanish historical press research. In this first stage, 143 titles published between 1772 and 1933 were included, amounting to 500,000 pages. Some of these pages were recovered from early attempts to digitize microfilms in 1997, such as *Semanario pintoresco español,* whereas other titles were digitized for inclusion in the new application.

Another goal was to establish cooperative partnerships with other institutions, by trying to complete fragmentary collections of serial titles and by sharing costs. Several digitization initiatives have been developed in Spain in recent years, some of them of great importance. It is worth mentioning here the *Biblioteca Virtual de Prensa Histórica,* funded by the Ministry of Culture of Spain, which includes historical titles of mainly journals and magazines held in Spanish public libraries, but which as of yet lacks OCR. It is accessible at http://hemerotecadigital.bne.es/recursos.htm. The Ministry has also mounted an OAI Directory that gathers basic information about existing digitization initiatives, using metadata harvesting techniques.

Standards

The standards followed in this project were developed in the previous digitization of the current press: 300 ppp minimal resolution, RGB color, and 256 level grey scale or black and white, depending on the publication. In addition to TIFF format master files, PDF encrypted multipage files, version 1.5 (accessible with Acrobat 6.X or higher) with JBIG2 compression in 150 ppp are generated to enable easy download from the Internet. All PDFs have thumbnails. OCR scanning is generated for each digitized page by the application ABBYY Fine Reader 9.0.

Due to the encryption of the PDF files, there is a list of restrictions:

- PDFs cannot be manipulated in any way;
- Single pages cannot be obtained from the PDF;
- Text cannot be copied;
- Images cannot be copied;
- Printing is allowed (at 150 dpi);
- Selection through an external software is allowed to facilitate accessibility to disabled people, but the text selected cannot be copied.

Every page has a semitransparent watermark with the inscription © Biblioteca Nacional de España.

Metadata is a question of great concern in the new project. The National Library is now analyzing which metadata are more suitable, in order to satisfy the constraints and requirements of its participation in the European Digital Library. At present, no decision has been made concerning which metadata will be mandatory, recommended or optional in the National Library. Since our metadata schema has not been defined yet, images in the Hemeroteca Digital have no metadata. Nevertheless, a database has been generated with the image directory and the data associated with them (in the form of technical or preservation data). This relational database is accessible through ODBC/JDBD standards. Files are structured in a directory with the following fields: title, year, month, day, number, page number, problems found during the digitization, TIFF images files, JPEG image files, as well as aspects related to format, compression algorithm, density of recording, access mode, etc. All this information will be incorporated to the metadata scheme that is finally chosen.

Workflow

Unfortunately, the National Library of Spain is not capable of developing such a tremendous enterprise on its own. Neither its premises nor its staff is large enough to undertake and maintain over the years the press digitization projects. It was thus necessary to outsource the project. We carefully analyzed all the tasks involved in order to guarantee the success of the digitization process. Steps taken in this regard are as follows:

- Collection of material. We have established certain security guidelines in order to protect the newspapers. There is a maximum number of volumes that can be carried in each vehicle, always keeping in mind scanner capacity. An insurance policy has been signed to cover transportation risks and the period of time that the documentation is housed at the contracted company. The policy's amount is determined by the Heritage Valuation Service of the National Library.
- Material collected must be kept in security packaging, and the vehicles used must be adapted to documentation transport. Both the National Library and the staff of the company supervise the packing and unpacking. A detailed delivery note or inventory is used to control delivery and later reception.
- Receipt of material. Once the company has the material, it checks the volumes and the delivery note and sends its conformity checklist to the National Library.
- Preparation. Bound volumes are checked for accuracy and information about dates, numbering, and pages is noted. It is strictly forbidden to unbind or cut pages. A sheet-by-sheet review is done to detect any physical damage: missing pages, tears, missing text, misarranged pages, poorly printed ones, stains, etc., or the presence of incorrect dates or numbers out of sequence. Digitization depth color is assigned at this stage.
- Image capture. Due to the fragility of these materials, scanners used are zenithal ones prepared to deal with oversized formats with color or prints. Volumes that need a more delicate treatment use scanners with central auxiliary lighting. If the page has some defect, it is corrected by image processing, if possible. Otherwise, the information is passed over to the database, to make sure that all flaws are properly

reported. When a page is missing, a blank image is inserted with the text "Missing page" or "Missing date".

- Digital image management. All images are checked, and those which do not comply with minimum quality standards are rejected and digitized again. After all the problems are resolved, files are renamed as JPEG and TIFF for the master file, and a record for each issue, with all the identification data and physical flaws found, is entered in a control database. Reports for each stage of the project are thereby generated.
- Recording medium. Master files are recorded in DVD-R in ISO 9669+UDF format.
- Return of the volumes to the National Library, which are checked against the delivery note. All safety measures must be followed.
- Optical character recognition process is made by ABBYY FINE READER 8.0 software, which has been successfully applied in the reading of periodicals images. This is a raw process, i.e., text obtained is not corrected in any way because otherwise it would be impossible to apply OCR to all the images.
- Collection generation: two PDF collections are generated, one in multipage PDF, made up by image and hidden text, and another one for the Web with watermarks and loss at 150 ppp.
- Server dump. Web image file collection is recorded in an external magnetic disc (HD), and after passing all checks it is dumped in the National Library of Spain Apache server. The indexing process begins immediately after, which is periodically checked. Once indexing is finished, titles are accessible at the Hemeroteca Digital.

These processes are carefully followed up. Quality control is an important issue for the National Library and reports are required at every step of the digitization process. Because this project is so expensive, we must make sure that outcomes meet all applicable standards.

Searching the Hemeroteca Digital

The Hemeroteca Digital can be accessed through the National Library home page, http://www.bne.es/ or directly at http://hemerotecadigital.bne.es/inicio.htm.

This is how the first screen looks: (see Figure 5.1 on page 58).

The first option, "Presentación", is a brief introduction to the scope, aims and selection criteria. The second option, "Consulta", allows users to start the search. The third option, "Otras hemerotecas digitales", provides information and links to other digital collections in Spain and makes the application a useful tool for anyone interested in searching or locating titles. A new option will soon be added, the "Listado de títulos" (list of titles), intended to simplify access for users and to facilitate our harvesting by external OAI servers.

Figure 5.1   Home page.

After clicking on "Consulta", the search screen opens: (see Figure 5.2 below).

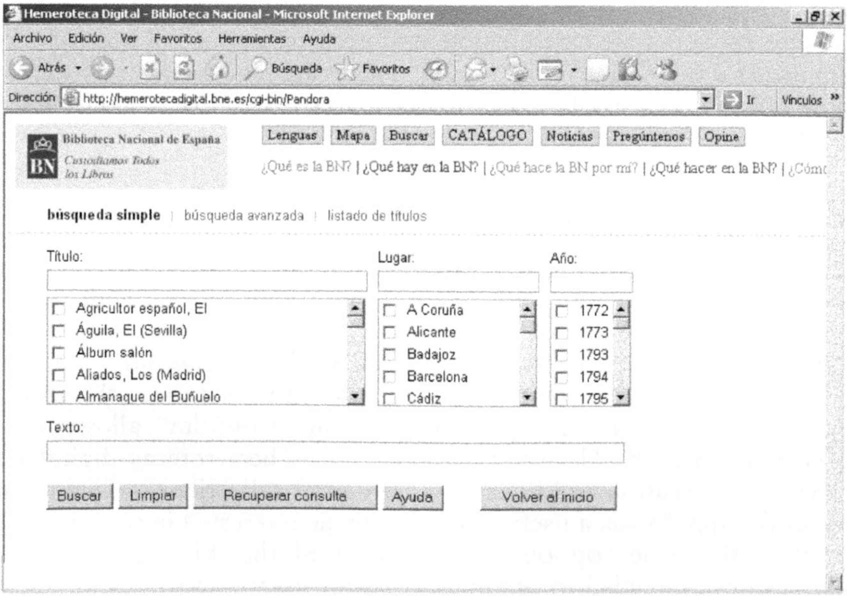

Figure 5.2   Search screen.

Browse

The browsing tool has two search aids to locate information: "búsqueda simple" (simple search) and "búsqueda avanzada" (advanced search). The first one has three indexes from which the elements can be selected: "título" (title), "lugar" (place) and "año" (year). The three can be combined together (see Figure 5.3 below).

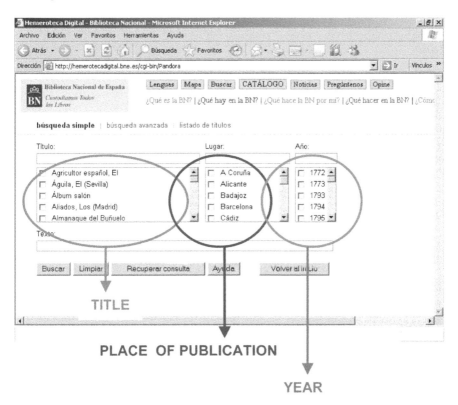

Figure 5.3   Simple search screen.

When the user selects a title, place of publication and dates are updated and show the information about the selected title. Once selected, the user must click on the search button ("Buscar") and the main page opens.

The system also allows full text searching, whether of the entire collection or by combining text search with the three indexes. This facility has made the Hemeroteca Digital an outstanding tool for using the press as a historical research source.

Besides these search options, the advanced search screen allows the user to establish search limits by date, either by locating a single date (for example, any given day) or a range of dates, or combining this capability with indexes of titles and places, and with a full text search. All these options are very useful when accurate searches are necessary, and reduce the amount of "false hits" (see Figure 5.4 below).

The results can also be sorted by relevance (the default order) or by date of publication, from the oldest to newest, or vice versa.

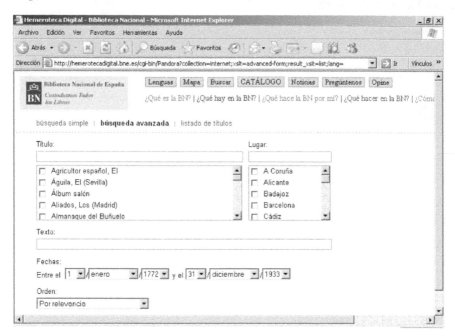

Figure 5.4　Advanced search screen.

Display

There are two display screens. The title display, in which the date has not been specified, looks as follows: (see Figure 5.5 on page 61).

This screen provides information about title, place, publication dates, and a brief history of the title. The link to the bibliographic record at the National Library catalog is always given and also other links to any other digital images known. This makes the application a very useful tool for researchers, who can view the copies held in other institutions and navigate through them.

The button "Mostrar Ejemplares" (display copies) opens another display screen: (see Figure 5.6 on page 61).

PDF files are opened from this screen, by clicking either the thumbnails or the blue PDF acronyms on the right. Information is given about the number of pages and the file size, and so the user can be apprised of the amount of time it will take to download the file. This is the screen that appears

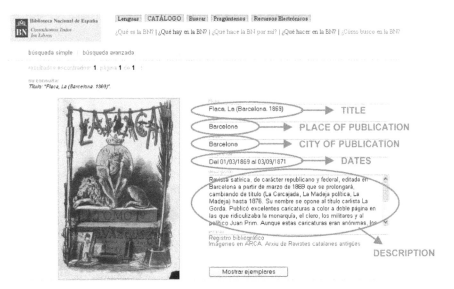

Figure 5.5 Title screen.

Figure 5.6 Title copies screen.

when a specific date or a term from the text is browsed. In case the entire information related to the title is needed, we can go back to the former screen by clicking on the blue title.

As mentioned earlier, there is always a link to the bibliographic record at the National Library's database, thus allowing for navigation between the digital collection and other formats available at the Library. It is also possible to change the display format of the bibliographic record and see an ISBD, labeled or MARC tagged format.

Clicking the link to the bibliographic record opens the connection with the OPAC, and from the new screen it is possible to navigate to the different formats available at the Library: (see Figures 5.7 to 5.10 on pages 62 to 64).

Text Search

Every page has been processed to extract text from an image using OCR, which allows for keyword searches. This is not a perfect tool, but anyone who has ever done research on the press will appreciate what a big improvement it actually is. Although the text is often misread due to the poor print quality of the papers in these years or because originals are in very poor condition, sometimes OCR retrieves good hits and is always useful as a means to look for clues, at the very least.

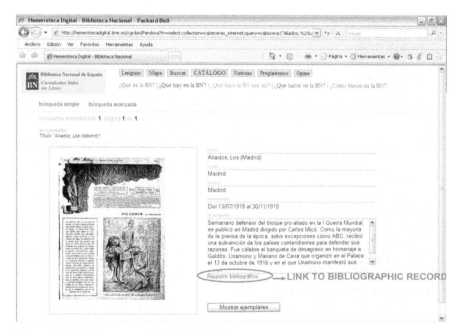

Figure 5.7   Link to record in the OPAC.

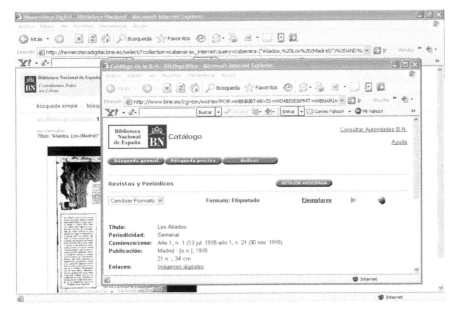

Figure 5.8 Record display in the OPAC.

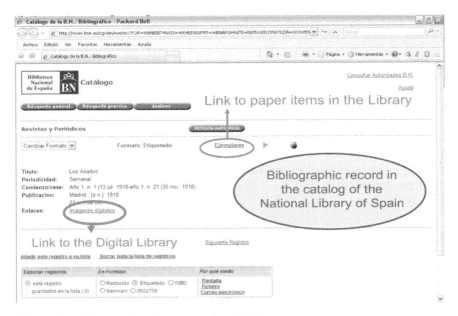

Figure 5.9 Link to digital images in the OPAC.

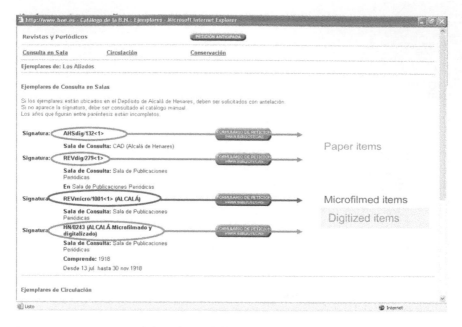

Figure 5.10 Formats of the title available at the library.

For example, if we are looking for information about Douglas Fairbanks, keying in "Fairbanks" in the text area results in twenty-five pages which are shown with the references to title, date, and file size. The noun searched is highlighted in yellow. Not all the hits relate to the famous American actor, but they are a good starting point for our investigation. From this screen it is possible to look at the entire page and use all the PDF tools to read it (zoom, page through issues, image rotation, etc.). Two examples are given below. The first one shows the presentation at Madrid's "Hipódromo" (Horse Racetrack) of artists Mary Pickford and Douglas Fairbanks to Queen Cristina of Spain during their visit to Madrid in June 1924, and the second one relates to the film premiere of "El Arréglalo Todo" (*Mr. Fix-It)* in November 1920 (see Figures 5.11 to 5.14 on pages 65 to 66).

Title List

A new search tool has been recently added, consisting of the list of all digitized titles arranged in alphabetical order with their place and dates of publication. This way, users can identify and better select titles at the beginning of the search (see Figure 5.15 on page 67).

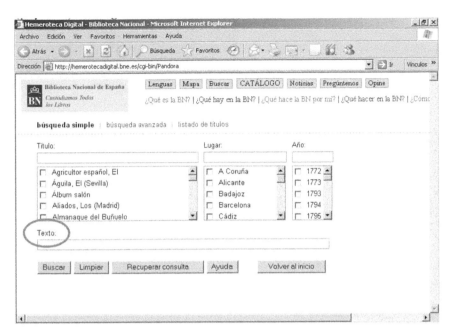

Figure 5.11 Keyword search.

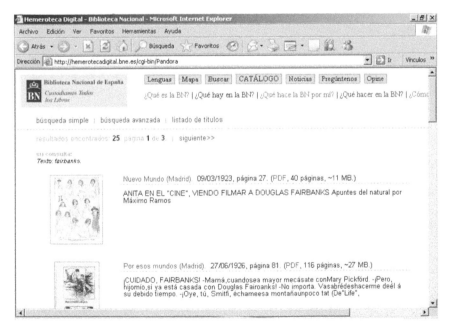

Figure 5.12 Page of results for Fairbanks.

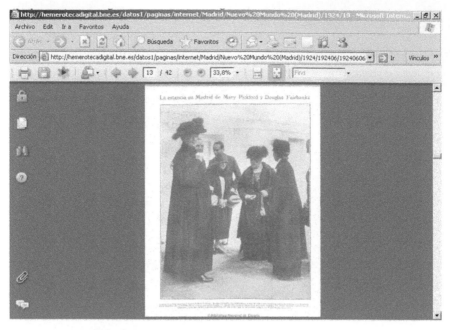

Figure 5.13   PDF screen. Example no. 1.

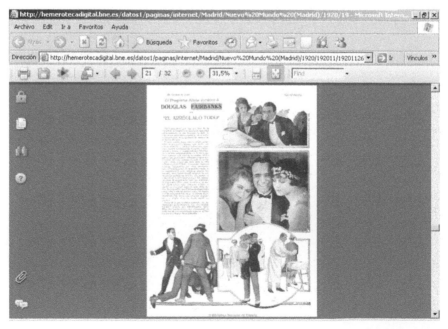

Figure 5.14   PDF screen. Example no. 2.

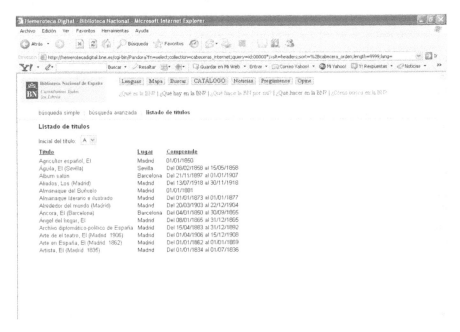

Figure 5.15   Title List.

Serving the Patrons

Taking these two digitization projects together (the Current Press and the Hemeroteca Digital), the Serials Department of the National Library of Spain now has 448 digitized titles and more than 35,000 CDs, which comprise about fifty million images, with a yearly growth of 4,000 CDs. To manage all the information available, digitized press research in our institution is now carried out in two ways, depending on the retrieval program that manages the title:

- Titles managed by the retrieval program on a Web platform developed for the National Library, which includes the titles mounted on the Internet (the Hemeroteca Digital) as well as those installed on the Intranet due to copyright constraints. This program has a capacity of five million pages in PDF with OCR;
- Titles managed by the retrieval program called "Visor Hemerográfico", not adapted for a Web platform, which has two applications: first, the server, which includes most frequently consulted titles that are copyright protected (*ABC, El País*) and the OCR of all the newspapers; and second, titles which have direct access through compact discs. This program now manages most newspaper titles of the 448 that have been digitized, but our intention is

to transfer as many as possible to the Intranet, a friendlier medium for users. The program must be installed on every workstation for press browsing purposes, but has the capability of serving a large number of workstations. Each of these workstations, in turn, has its own printer and card-operated reader that enables the user to obtain paper copies of all the information desired.

Therefore, for the time being, users interested in research on the current press must come to the National Library themselves, while research on older material can be done, at least in part, from outside the library.

To make searching easier for users, a new press search tool has been mounted on the Web page of the National Library of Spain. It consists of a database of all microfilmed or digitized serial titles accessible at the Library, and has been designed independently from the OPAC in order to simplify searches centered on surrogate serials. This database, called "Prensa digitalizada y microfilmada" can be consulted at the Serial Reading Room Web page at the following URL: http://www.bne.es/esp/servicios/salapp.htm. Nevertheless, as we mentioned earlier, the information remains also in the bibliographic or holdings record of the catalog.

Some Statistics

The figures below show an overview of the usage statistics of the Hemeroteca Digital since April, 2007:

Table 5.1   Monthly usage statistics.

Month	Monthly totals				
	Volume	*Visits*	*Pages*	*Files*	*Hits*
Aug. 2007	757.43 Gb	10337	66981	356818	767071
July 2007	244.23 Gb	9865	65960	346197	601230
June 2007	254.31 Gb	11003	74290	386041	665895
May 2007	351.45 Gb	14423	107749	545374	893893
April 2007	362.56 Gb	13416	92579	471546	836791
Total	1.96 Tb	59044	407559	2105976	3764880

Lastly, it must be stressed that the users of the National Library appreciate the effort made to support their research, as evidenced by several opinion surveys and shown in the figures comparing the use of the digital collection and of other formats in the Serials Reading Room:

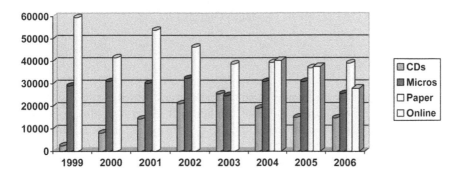

Figure 5.16 Usage statistics by formats for the period 1999 to 2006 on a yearly basis.

This figure refers to all kinds of serial publications (i.e., magazines, journals, newspapers, etc.) provided in the Serials Reading Room. The category "online" refers only to those newspaper titles mounted on the server in 2004, namely *El País* and *ABC*.

Future Developments

The issues addressed so far focused on the first stage of the application. However, we must bear in mind that the project is an ongoing one. Thus, for the period of 2007 to 2009, the digitization of 3,700,000 new images will be accomplished. This will cover the most relevant titles of the seventeenth, eighteenth and nineteenth centuries. Emphasis will be on titles of the Spanish Independence War (1808–1814), whose commemoration will soon take place. As to press history, this is a very rich period in which a huge number of short-lived titles were published, and the National Library collections are unique in this regard. All the images coming from microfilm digitization will be exhaustively checked, in order to facilitate OCR reading.

At the same time, the ongoing current press digitization program will proceed, and the local network will allow browsing these titles at the Library site. As mentioned earlier, they cannot be mounted on the Internet due to copyright restrictions.

Our next steps will be as follows. First, to increase as much as possible the number of digitized titles and digitized pages. Before the end of 2008, we will have digitized 3,700,000 new pages of older titles, and we will continue digitizing the current press on a yearly basis, at about 2,500,000 pages each year. Second, to integrate this collection—at least on the title level—into the OAI server of Hispanic Digital Library.

CONCLUSIONS

The two projects addressed in this article, microfilming and digitizing, allow the National Library, head of the Spanish library system, to supply surrogate copies of its collections to any institution interested. The institution pays only for reproduction. In this way, duplication of efforts and costs are avoided, and the aim of joining forces and identifying collections is achieved.

The project has yielded two main benefits for the National Library facilities:

- Benefits in conservation matters: as stated before, although conservation was not the main objective of the program, digitization has proved to have had a great impact on the newspaper collection. One copy of the current newspapers received through legal deposit is kept in acid-free cardboard boxes and stored flat in the stacks. Consequently, originals are preserved in perfect condition, avoiding any manipulations (trimming, binding) and protecting them from environmental agents which could damage the physical medium, such as dust, humidity or microorganisms. Furthermore, keeping both old and current newspaper collections out of circulation prevents damage caused by use, which is the most important factor that leads to their deterioration. Having a digital collection in reserve, or master copy, is an additional benefit, and if necessary, it could be used for duplication without touching the originals again.
- Benefits in information access: As we have already mentioned, due to the lack of space in the stacks of the main site of the National Library, the Recoletos building, the press was housed off-site in the second stacks area at Alcalá de Henares, near Madrid. As a consequence, users had to make a written request and wait for a day before consulting the press. In addition, before the digitization project was undertaken, newspapers were bound for the sake of preservation, thus delaying the availability of current titles which were "in the bindery". Consequently, although most important titles could be consulted at other libraries, users' frustration was considerable. Furthermore, press research has experienced important growth in recent years, and quite often a publication could not be consulted by a user because it had been supplied to another user, or because the title was being reproduced at the Reprographic Department of the Library at a patron's request. All these factors ended up making titles unavailable for the disappointed users.

Digitization has considerably reduced the amount of time in which newspapers are made available. Digital images are networked, and can simultaneously be browsed by several users who can print or download whatever they want at the printers located at every workstation.

OCR also allows full text searching and compensates for the lack of press indexes or analytics [very useful tools for locating information in serial publications]. OCR plays this role and thus provides an added value to digitization.

By way of conclusion, we would like to stress our desire that the new Hemeroteca Digital will make a relevant contribution in supporting remote access to our collections, thereby promoting the research and dissemination of our historical and cultural heritage. The project not only aims at promoting access to digital images, but it also intends to compile all digital resources related to the Spanish press and to provide all the links available, thereby offering a most complete tool for researchers.

NOTES

Other resources and links at the National Library of Spain related to the serials collection:

1. Electronic address: Hemeroteca Digital has an e-mail for comments or questions from users at hemerotecadigital@bne.es.
2. Spanish Press on the Internet Directory: the Reference Department at the National Library compiles and keeps up to date all the Spanish newspaper URLs on the Internet. This directory is now available at http://www.bne.es/esp/servicios/prensainternet.htm.
3. The database with all microfilmed and digitized titles accessible at the National Library can be consulted at http://www.bne.es/esp/catalogos/buscon.htm.
4. Electronic resources: press and periodicals search is completed by subscription to full text databases, which include the most important international titles. A simple tool has been designed for consulting these purchased titles at: http://www.bne.es/esp/servicios/recursos_electronicos.htm.

6 GIS Technology as an Alternative Way of Access to Historical Knowledge

Albina Moscicka
Translated by Alla Makeeva-Roylance

INTRODUCTION

Fundamentals of Geographic Information Systems

A geographic information system (GIS) is a system for capturing, storing, managing, processing and displaying the data spatially referenced to the surface of the Earth. Generally speaking, the complete geographic information system requires, first of all, hardware, software and data as well as a set of procedures for data management and analysis. It also demands personnel who are able to plan, implement and use a system as well as meaningfully interpret the collected data.

The essence of GIS functioning rests in its ability to integrate data from diverse sources in diverse formats into a single cohesive database of geographical information. Such a database contains information on geographical locations on the surface of the Earth or natural phenomena, recognizes relationships between them and includes information on their attributes and characteristics. Because of the advanced functions of the data analysis and display, the information collected though GIS methods enables a better knowledge and comprehension of the relationships and laws which govern the real world. Therefore, a GIS system can simultaneously serve as a depository of spatial information and as a collection of functions necessary to interpret and manipulate the data. A GIS must be distinguished from other information systems chiefly based on its use of technology that allows a complex analysis of spatial data and related attributes which results in a presentation of this analysis in a cartographic form, in other words, in the form of maps.

The development of a GIS involves transferring the elements of the real world onto a computer monitor by means of models and symbols which can be interpreted by an information system. This multiphase process requires familiarity with the processes and phenomena of the real world. A functional GIS requires:

- Development of a conceptual model, i.e., defining the scope of spatial and topical data and the method of their presentation;
- Development of a logical model, i.e., the identification of a fragment of the real world and its description by means of a set of commands understood by a computer;
- Development of a physical model, i.e., working directly with the architecture of the database;
- Implementation, i.e., the collection and analysis of the data, and finally, the presentation of results.

Geographical data used by a GIS describes objects which can be referenced to the surface of the Earth. Every object can be described by a set of attributes which may be of a spatial nature (the location of an object, its shape, topographical connections between objects, etc.) or it may be of a nonspatial nature (characteristic features, values). The spatial attributes of an object, or its geometrical characteristics and location, can be represented by a pair of x, y coordinates (point features) or by a sequence of pairs of x, y coordinates (linear and area features) within a given frame of reference. Objects may also possess an attribute of elevation (e.g., relief) which can be annotated by the third coordinate, z. Nonspatial attributes of geographic objects can be of a quantitative (number, value) and/or qualitative (category) nature and they are determined by a specific field of knowledge for which a GIS is being developed.

Many spatial objects and phenomena change with time. Their shape, size and location as well as their descriptive attributes can be subjected to permutation. In geographic information systems time is considered an additional attribute and can be represented by yet another, t coordinate. The issues related to the four-dimensional data models of (x,y,z,t) are the most fundamental problems of contemporary geoinformatics.

The Purpose of the Project

A system of spatial information allows storing, managing and presenting spatial data which can undergo changes with time. Therefore, it is possible, with the help of a GIS, to accumulate historical information and have it presented on a map. The very nature of historic events is that they unfold over the course of time and can happen in different locations of the geographic space. Therefore, it is necessary to define when and where a given historical event occurred. Historical events are typical examples of a spatiotemporal phenomenon.

Biblical events can also be understood as spatiotemporal historical events. Currently, the book market offers scores of works, including cartographic ones, related to the Bible and Biblical geography. An analysis of these works yields the fact that all the events are described more or less similarly. Meanwhile, there is a wide disparity in the representation of Biblical objects on maps found in Biblical research documents. These differences stem from the object onomastics as well as localization within the geographic space. Sometimes different maps (often in works put out by the same publisher) place the same object in different locations or under different names. This results in erroneous positioning of events in the geographic space which in turn can result in improper interpretation of the Biblical events.

It is important to remember that the precise knowledge of Biblical geography is a cornerstone of the reconstruction and understanding of events in the Bible. The occurrences described in the Bible are connected to the geographic locales which have undergone changes in the course of millennia. These changes may have occurred in the location of geographic entities (e.g., the destruction of a city and its rebuilding at a different location) as well as its name (e.g., a city was renamed in the course of history). The geographic objects in the Bible and events related to these locations are typical examples of phenomena occurring both in time and space.

This project, sponsored by the Ministry of Science and Higher Education and undertaken by the Institute of Geodesy and Cartography (Warsaw, Poland), together with the Jagiellonian University (Cracow, Poland) and the Cardinal Stefan Wyszynski University (Warsaw, Poland), aims to develop a spatiotemporal system of geographic information related to historic events and the relevant sources of the historic information. The main purpose of the project is to develop a step-by-step methodology and to implement a time-oriented information system which is based on events described in the Bible and which derives information from the maps of the Old and New Testaments.

We hope that the system at work will be used by Biblical scholars who will be able to supply thematic content, create time-space juxtapositions and conduct analyses and comparisons. We also hope that it can be used for educational purposes and will be able to display information on Biblical events in an attractive manner.

The proposed GIS is expected to contain both a reference database and a subject database.

The reference database contains information on the geographic locales which over the course of thousands of years have not undergone changes (or changed the least). It is generally accepted that such elements are the relief of a terrain (represented as a shaded numbered model of a terrain) and hydrology. The reference database will generate a basemap which will be shared by all subject maps.

Subject databases contain information essential for the representation of specific Biblical events, among them: geographic objects which appear in the Bible, regions populated by certain tribes, migration routes, etc. Biblical events will be presented on the backdrop of the reference map, which will be supplemented by facts relevant to a given theme, i.e., by the geographic features typical for the time period during which a Biblical event occurred and which are significant in regard to this event.

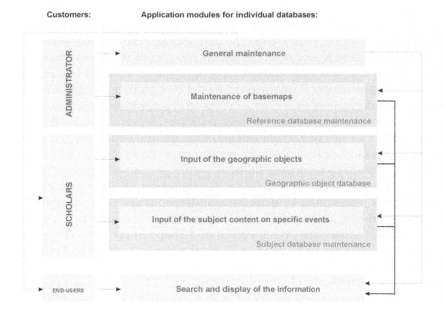

Figure 6.1   Schema of the System.

The databases will be served by means of an Internet application (Fig. 6.1) which will employ several separate modules, designated for and utilized by different groups of users:

- An administrator will service an administrative module and a module governing the reference database;
- Biblical scholars (researchers) will input relevant information into the subject databases;
- Users will study the source and create visual representations.

PROPOSED SOLUTION

A Spatiotemporal Model of a Biblical Geographic Object

Historical information recorded in a GIS requires that three components of a given phenomenon be defined: place, time and an array of attributes. Unfortunately, GIS packages currently available on the market do not possess features that allow representation of time-specific events. This is due to the fact that there are serious conceptual shortcomings in an informational model of a GIS which create obstacles for capturing the time element. Therefore, GIS specialists have a free hand in their approach to representing spatiotemporal information in a GIS. This can be perceived as an additional difficulty in preparing a GIS; however, it also gives scholars freedom to propose adequate solutions relevant to their area of research and particulars of their data, without trying to adapt their research to the limitations of the existing software.

Thus, an effective recording of the information about the events which are changeable in time and space demands a geographic information system that will have a spatiotemporal information model built in its software architecture. The development of such a model relies on describing the structure of the data—through the specifications of basic principles, acceptable visual models and connections—in a way which will allow the use and visual representation of this information, depending on the needs and purposes of the system.

When it comes to recording Biblical events, it is an accepted practice that, in a designed system, the ability of geographic objects to change in time-space is represented by defining simultaneous states of the objects, i.e., their shapes at distinct periods of time. Within the same time period (or within the same date), the position and shape of the objects as well as their attributes are to be defined. A spatiotemporal object will consist of its many time-relevant states and, consequently, a variety of shapes, locations and attributes changeable with time. Therefore, the development of a spatiotemporal model of a Biblical object demands that the principles and patterns of the variability of features of an object in time are clearly defined.

Let's assume that a spatiotemporal geographic object O is a geographic object which is mentioned in the Bible and which, during different periods of time T, could have different locations or attributes. The shape of a given geographic object, i.e., a defined geographic position together with attributes in a random i-th time period, can be recorded as the state S of the object within that time period (Fig. 6.2).

Furthermore, any j-th spatiotemporal geographic object O_j can be represented as a sum of the states of the object S_i in given time periods T_i.

$$O_j = \bigcup_{i=1}^{n} S_i \; ,$$

[1]

where n is a number of states of the j-th geographic object.

The state of a geographic object within a given time period can be defined as an instantaneous state of an object (Fig. 6.3). Any instantaneous state of an object can be defined as:

$$S_i = S(T_i),$$

[2]

where T_i is the j-th time period, for which we determine the state of the geographic object S_i.

Thus, the spatiotemporal geographic object O_j, represented by the formula [1] can be recorded as:

$$O_j = \bigcup_{i=1}^{n} S_i = \bigcup_{i=1}^{n} S(T_i) \quad , \tag{3}$$

The instantaneous state of the object can consist of the geographic location P of the object as well as its attributes A. These attributes can be either stable or modifiable.

Either a geographic object $A^{st}(O_j)$ or the state of the object $A^{st}(T_j)$ can possess stable attributes A^{st}. Thus the stable attributes of the j-th geographic object can be recorded as:

$$A_j^{st} = \bigcup_{i=1}^{n} A^{st}(T_i) + A^{st}(O_j) \quad , \tag{4}$$

One of the stable attributes for a given state of an object, i.e., unchangeable within a given time period, is the name of the geographic object N, which can be defined for the i-th time period as:

$$N_i = N(T_i), \tag{5}$$

In most cases, the name of the object remains the same in several (or all) states of the geographic object.

The stable attributes for each geographic object $A^{st}(O_j)$ in all states are:

- a category of the geographic object R, which for the j-th geographic object is defined as:

$$R_j = R(O_j), \tag{6}$$

- its location in the Bible L_j, i.e., where the geographic object O_j is mentioned in the Holy Scriptures, with an indication as to whether it appears in the Old or New Testament, the name of the book, and the chapter and verse.

Therefore, the attribute L_j is a collection of all locations of the given geographic object in the Bible. A basic k-th localization of the j-th geographic object in the Bible can be represented as:

$$L_{k,j} = L_k(O_j), \tag{7}$$

whereas the collection of the localizations of the j-th geographic object in the Bible can be represented as:

$$L_j = \bigcup_{k=1}^{n} L_{k,j} = \bigcup_{k=1}^{n} L_k(O_j) \quad , \tag{8}$$

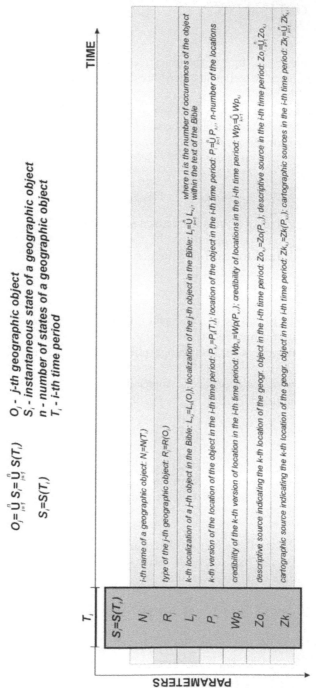

Figure 6.2   A model of a geographic time sensitive object.

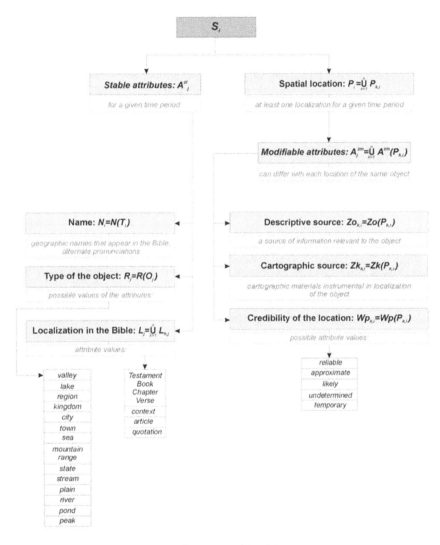

Figure 6.3 Instantaneous state of a geographic object.

where n is the number of the occurrences of the localization of the j-th geographic object in the Bible.

Bearing in mind the formulae [4]-[8], it can be recorded that:

$$A^{st}_{i} = A^{st}(T_{i})=N_{i}=N(T_{i}) \text{ for a state of the object,} \qquad [9]$$

whereas for the j-th object:

$$\bigcup_{i=1}^{n} A^{st}(T_{i})=\bigcup_{i=1}^{n} N_{i}=\bigcup_{i=1}^{n} N(T_{i})$$

$$A^{st}(O_{j})=R_{j}+L_{j}=R_{j}+\bigcup_{k=1}^{n} L_{k,j}=R(O_{j})+\bigcup_{k=1}^{n} L_{k}(O_{j}) \quad , \qquad [10]$$

or:

$$A^{st}_{j}=\bigcup_{i=1}^{n} A^{st}(T_{i})+A^{st}(O_{j})=\bigcup_{i=1}^{n} N_{i}+R_{j}+L_{j}=\bigcup_{i=1}^{n} N_{i}+R_{j}+\bigcup_{k=1}^{n} L_{k,j}=\bigcup_{i=1}^{n} N(T_{i})+R(O_{j})+\bigcup_{k=1}^{n} L_{k}(O_{j})$$

$$[11]$$

Modifiable attributes A_{j}^{zm} of the geographic object depend on a version where the object is assumed to be located in a given time period. The descriptive and cartographic sources are of critical importance for the final project because the information about the object and its spatial location, as well as the credibility of these locations, is drawn from them.

The spatiotemporal geographic object can possess several hypothetical versions of its location within one given time period (or for one state of the object). The basic k-th version of the spatial location in the i-th time period can be represented as:

$$P_{k,i}=P_{k}(T_{i}), \qquad [12]$$

whereas the collection of the locations of that object in the framework of the state of the object is defined as

$$P_{i}=\bigcup_{k=1}^{n} P_{k,i}=\bigcup_{k=1}^{n} P_{k}(T_{i}), \qquad [13]$$

where n is the number of the hypothetical locations of the geographic object in the i-th time period.

Modifiable attributes A_{j}^{zm} of the geographic object, dependent on the version of its location, are:

credibility of the spatial location of the geographic object Wp; credibility of the k-th version of the location in the i-th time period can be recorded as:

$$WP_{k,i} = Wp(P_{k,i}) = Wp(P_k(T_i)),$$ [14]

whereas the credibility of locations in the i-th time period is:

$$Wp_i = \bigcup_{k=1}^{n} Wp_{k,i} = \bigcup_{k=1}^{n} Wp(P_{k,i}) = \bigcup_{k=1}^{n} Wp(P_k(T_i)),$$ [15]

descriptive source which provided the information about the object and versions of its location Zo; descriptive source which indicates k-th location of the object in the i-th time period can be recorded as:

$$Zo_{k,i} = Zo(P_{k,i}) = Zo(P_k(T_i)),$$ [16]

whereas descriptive sources in the i-th time period are:

$$Zo_i = \bigcup_{k=1}^{n} Zo_{k,i} = \bigcup_{k=1}^{n} Zo(P_{k,i}) = \bigcup_{k=1}^{n} Zo(P_k(T_i)),$$ [17]

cartographic source Zk, based on which the location of the object was determined; a cartographic source which identifies the k-th location of the object in the i-th time periods can be recorded as:

$$Zk_{k,i} = Zk(P_{k,i}) = Zk(P_k(T_i)),$$ [18]

whereas cartographic sources in the i-th time period are:

$$Zk_i = \bigcup_{k=1}^{n} Zk_{k,i} = \bigcup_{k=1}^{n} Zk(P_{k,i}) = \bigcup_{k=1}^{n} Zk(P_k(T_i));$$ [19]

Furthermore, bearing in mind the formulae [12]-[19], the collection of the modifiable attributes of the spatiotemporal j-th geographic object can be recorded as:

$$A_j^{zm} = \bigcup_{k=1}^{n} A^{zm}(P_{k,i}),$$ [20]

$$A_j^{zm} = \bigcup_{k=1}^{n} [Wp_{k,i} + Zo_{k,i} + Zk_{k,i}]$$ [21]

$$A_j^{zm} = \bigcup_{k=1}^{n} \left[Wp(P_{k,i}) + Zo(P_{k,i}) + Zk(P_{k,i}) \right] \qquad [22]$$

$$A_j^{zm} = \bigcup_{k=1}^{n} \left[Wp(P_k(T_i)) + Zo(P_k(T_i)) + Zk(P_k(T_i)) \right], \qquad [23]$$

Taking into consideration the stable and modifiable attributes as well as the location of the geographic object (formulae [4]-[23]), an instantaneous state of the object can be recorded as:

$$S_i = S(T_i), \qquad [24]$$

$$s_i = A_j^{st} + A_j^{zm} + P_i, \qquad [25]$$

$$S_i = A^{st}(T_i) + A^{st}(O_j) + \bigcup_{k=1}^{n} \left[Wp_{k,i} + Zo_{k,i} + Zk_{k,i} \right] + P_i, \qquad [26]$$

$$S_i = N_i + R_j + L_j + \bigcup_{k=1}^{n} \left[Wp(P_{k,i}) + Zo(P_{k,i}) + Zk(P_{k,i}) \right] + \bigcup_{k=1}^{n} P_{k,i}, \qquad [27]$$

$$S_i = N(T_i) + R(O_j) + \bigcup_{i=k}^{n} L_k(O_j) + \bigcup_{k=1}^{n} \left[Wp(P_k(T_i)) + Zo(P_k(T_i)) + Zk(P_k(T_i)) \right] + \bigcup_{k=1}^{n} P_k(T_i),$$

$$[28]$$

Based on the formula [28], a spatiotemporal geographic object can be represented as:

$$O_j = \bigcup_{i=1}^{n} S_i = \bigcup_{i=1}^{n} \left[N(T_i) + R(O_j) + \bigcup_{k=1}^{n} L_k(O_j) + \bigcup_{k=1}^{n} \left[Wp(P_k(T_i)) + Zo(P_k(T_i)) + Zk(P_k(T_i)) \right] + \bigcup_{k=1}^{n} P_k(T_i) \right]$$

$$[29]$$

The above model of a spatiotemporal object serves as a foundation for defining the kind of features of the object and in which way it can be acquired for the system. These deliberations also allow us to draw conclusions about the interdependence of individual attributes. Therefore, the development of the spatial information system requires the implementation of the informational model, described in this chapter.

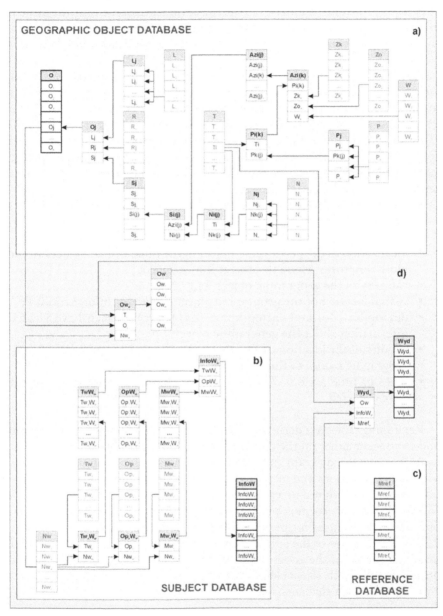

Figure 6.4   Architecture of the system.

Input Data

A spatiotemporal information system with a focus on Biblical events consists of three distinct databases. Therefore, the development of the system architecture (Fig. 6.4, 6.5) requires that all its elements have their respective structures defined and the connections among the individual databases established.

A spatiotemporal model of a geographic object is a key element in the structural development of the database dedicated to the geographic objects in the Bible (Fig. 6.4a). Implementation of the spatiotemporal model of a geographic object involves development of a table blueprint which contains information on all components of Biblical geographic objects: their spatial location, time element and attributes. The interconnections and relationships among individual tables should also be defined. Figure 6.4a represents the suggested architecture of the geographic object database. Data which can be directly entered into the database are highlighted. This information includes:

- localization of the geographic object in the Bible (*L*), i.e., places in the Holy Scriptures where the object is mentioned;
- category of the geographic object *R*;
- spatial location of the geographic object (geometry information) *P*;
- descriptive *(Zo)* and cartographic *(Zk)* sources, which have yielded information about the geographic object;
- validity of the location of the object *W*;
- geographic names of the object *N*;
- dates or time periods *T*, when a name change or a location change have occurred.

Remaining tables are derivative and contain data which was pre-selected and contingent either on the category of the object *j* or the time period *i*.

Arrows on the diagram indicate relationships among individual tables. They define directions and methods of using individual attributes, depending on how they are assigned to a given object *j* and/or a given time period *i*. Such solution makes possible multiple uses for objects with similar (recurring) attributes, without the need for repetitive entry of data or its duplication.

The architecture of the subject database shown in figure 6.4b is similar in design to that of the geographic object database. Marked in red are the primary tables with those elements which need to be entered in the database directly. Such elements are:

- names of the events *Nw*;
- courses of the events *Tw*;
- descriptions of the events *Op*;
- multimedia content of the events *Mw*.

GEOGRAPHIC OBJECT DATABASE:

W—validity of a geographic object location
Zo—descriptive source, on the basis of which the information of a geographic object was obtained
Zk—cartographic source, on the basis of which a geographic object was localized
P—location of a geographic object
Pj—location of a j-th geographic object
Pk(j)—primary k-th location of a j-th geographic object
Pi(k)—primary k-th location of a geographic object in the i-th time period
T—time (collection of dates/time periods)
Ti—i-th time period
Azi(k)—modifiable attributes of primary k-th location of a geographic object in the i-th time period
Azi(j)—set of modifiable attributes of the j-th geographic object in the i-th time period
N—names of geographic objects
Nj—name of the j-th geographic object
Nk(j)—primary k-th name of the j-th geographic object
Ni(j)—names of the j-th geographic object in the i-th time period
Si(j) - state of the j-th geographic object in the i-th time period
Sj—set of instantaneous states of the j-th geographic object
R—categories of geographic objects
Rj—category of the j-th geographic object
I—localizations of geographic objects in the Bible
Lj - localizations of the j-th geographic object in the Bible
Oj—j-th geographic object
O—geographic object database

SUBJECT DATABASE:

Nw—name of a topical event
Nw$_w$—name of the w-th topical event
Tw—routes (or other geometric objects) of topical events
Tw$_x$—primary x-th route of a topical event
Op—descriptions (or other textual data) of a topical event
Op$_x$—primary x-th description of a topical event
Mw—multimedia content on a topical events
Mw$_x$—primary x-th multimedia data of a topical event
Tw$_x$W$_w$—primary x-th route of the w-th topical event
Op$_x$W$_w$—primary x-th description of the w-th topical event
Mw$_x$W$_w$—primary x-th multimedia data on the w-th topical event
TwW—set of routes of the w-th topical events
OpW$_w$—set of descriptions of the w-th topical event
MwW$_w$—mulitmedia set for the w-th topical event
InfoW$_w$—set of topical information on the w-th topical event
InfoW—subject database of topical events

REFERENCE DATABASE:

Mref—reference map database
Mref$_w$—reference map for the w-th topical event

Miscellaneous:

Ow$_w$—primary geographic object relevant to the w-th topical event
Ow$_w$—set of geographic objects relevant to the w-th topical event
Wyd$_w$—package of data necessary for representation of the w-th topical event
Wyd—topical event database

Figure 6.5 Legend of the system architecture.

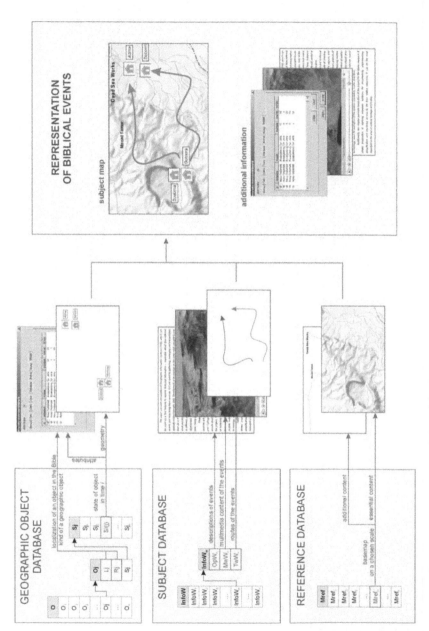

Figure 6.6   Representation of the Biblical Event.

Arrows indicate how individual names of the events are related to the routes of the events, their descriptions and related multimedia, thus creating a complete set of subject data on a specific Biblical event $InfoW_w$.

The structure of the reference database (Fig. 6.4c) differs somewhat from other databases. The reference database contains only basemaps $Mref$ of different scales; on their background, the Biblical events on a specific subject can be represented. The elements of this database are divided into two categories:

- primary elements: numerical model of the terrain and hydrography;
- secondary elements: current situational content.

The architecture of a spatiotemporal information system about Biblical events rests on the structures of the three databases described above. It is also enhanced with information on the relations and interdependence among the individual databases (Fig. 6.4d). A given name of an event Nw_w from the geographic database is attributed with a set of geographic objects Ow, which, in connection with the set of subject information on the $InfoW_w$, represents an event Wyd_w on the background of a chosen reference map $Mref_w$. Thus, the database of the Biblical events contains sets of cartographic and descriptive information on thematic events.

OUTPUT DATA

According to the stated purpose and principles of the project, the end result will be a product which will allow the representation of Biblical events on maps. Figure 6.6 demonstrates the method and the pattern of representation of an event to a user. The diagram shows all three databases that comprise the spatial information system as well as specific information on a given topic, collected from each of these databases.

The database of geographic objects supplies information on attributes of geographic objects relevant to a given event, as well as the states of these objects (i.e., their shape) at the time when the event occurred.

Information of the route of a given event, its description as well as its multimedia elements which allow representation of the event, are drawn from the subject database.

The basemap relevant to the category of the event and its scope comes from the reference database.

Geometric information (basemap, routes of the events, geographic objects) selected from these databases allows the development of the subject map of a Biblical event. Attributes, description and multimedia are combined to provide additional information which leads to a deeper understanding of the event presented on that map. These types of information, first of all, enable a user to establish the localization of the event in the

Bible (quotations make it possible to pinpoint where in the Bible and how a given event is described); they also refer a user to different descriptive and cartographic sources (which often provide an alternative interpretation of the same events).

An additional bonus from the localization of Biblical events in time and space is that they provide a foundation for reports and comparisons; they also allow for the construction of inquiries and spatiotemporal analyses. Among other tasks, it is possible to:

- retrieve information on geographic objects which appear in the area of interest in the given time period;
- retrieve information on geographic objects which appear in a given book of the Holy Scriptures;
- retrieve information on the Biblical events which took place in a given area or during a given time period;
- compile combinations of names of the geographic objects during a given time period.

Technology

As mentioned earlier, the current market offers limited a choice of GIS software which takes the time element into consideration, therefore it was decided to employ programming technologies for incorporating the solutions into Web pages.

The proposed application which administers the system consists of two parts: the server application and the client application. The server application is designed by means of PHP scripts, but can also utilize other kinds of scripts as well (jsp, asp, etc.). The client application is programmed in the Flash scripting language, ActionScript.

The source data are stored on a server as binary files. Map data are prepared as square matrices which makes possible the hidden use of vector data. Such a solution allows a significant compression of information and, consequently, a reduction in the amount of transferred information. The square matrix arrangement guarantees that only small amounts of data are being searched at the same time, thus making the query response time relatively short. With the help of such popular GIS formats as SHP (ArcView) or TAB (MapInfo) it is possible to generate the data within minutes. It allows preparing the data for the development of a GIS, and later for transferring it to a Web application.

The client-server application functions in the following manner:

1. The address of the map is entered, i.e., a user selects a map of interest.
2. The server forwards a startup application to a user.
3. A startup application sends a request for an appropriate application to the server.

4. The server forwards the appropriate application.
5. The application forwards a request for the initial information and a selected map fragment.
6. Subsequent map fragments are forwarded upon request from the user.
7. The square matrices, which were sent at the user's request, are registered in the local Flash memory; the application utilizes them locally, sending an additional request only for missing parts.
8. The search results and additional information are retrieved at the request of the user.

The principal advantage of such a solution is the lack of interdependence among the database environments on the server; it makes possible the minimal use of equipment, while the source data are prepared in such a way that a search on the request of the client application brings very quick results. The average response time on a designated server which stores several different servers and maps, is less than 0.01 second (with a Pentium D 3.4 GHz processor with the memory capacity of 2GB).

POSSIBLE USAGE OF THE PROPOSED SOLUTION IN CULTURAL HERITAGE STUDIES

A map is the most effective method of representing spatially referenced data. The majority of GIS packages allow easy and speedy development of maps which are based on spatial data aggregated in a GIS. Such maps can be prepared multiple times and refined in the course of research so that the most accurate representation of facts can be achieved.

The significance of spatial information, both in terms of access and presentation of digitally preserved information from the accumulated resources of cultural heritage, is often underestimated. All too often, exceptionally valuable efforts to bring cultural heritage materials to a user are not consistent. While preserving historic monuments in a digital form, we often focus on "what" and "how much" we have, and tend to forget that "where" and "what location" is relevant to our digital reserves. User demands grow steadily. Some of them are satisfied with a simple image on a monitor, others go online in search of information and the location with which this information is associated. In both cases, the ability to accurately locate pertinent materials (including those of geographic spatial nature) is crucial.

Access to the digital collections of a cultural heritage, which are aggregated and arranged in a form of catalogs, is undoubtedly a very effective way to use available materials. However, in order to find an object of scientific interest it is necessary to browse through many individual catalogs, which can be time-consuming. Inconsistencies in accumulated resources and incongruity of standards in organizing various catalogs make the task especially laborious; the difficulty in precise placement of an object within a geographic space often prevents a user from finding the objects in the geographic area of research. Use of a GIS facilitates the access to cultural heritage treasures by allowing the sorting and retrieval of information by means of integrated subject, time, and geographic criteria, which, in turn, leads to a fuller picture on a subject of research.

Well-understood spatial information can serve as common ground for the integration of diverse initiatives related to easier access to the cultural heritage information. Systems of spatial information make possible not only integration of multitudes of scattered databases and simultaneous presentation of their contents, but also allow the aggregation of descriptive data from these databases. Thus, they provide a user with a set of solutions and tools for the localization of the subject of interest in a geographic space, as well as with wealth of additional information.

Geoinformational technologies are perfect in providing access to a range of various online collections from a single common level, i.e., from a map. A map prepared in accordance with the laws of the cartographic art is an exceptionally expressive medium. It depicts spatial relations in a most immediate way, as a direct image of these relations in reality. A small space of a map can contain so much information that it would require several pages to describe it verbally. What's more, a small map image can spur many intellectual endeavors which can lead to heterogeneous conclusions. Maps allow a more effective processing of information, and can make the memorization process easier, faster and more enjoyable which without doubt will support multidirectional creative thinking.

For anyone who observes currently available systems it is hard to miss one observation: they focus mostly on historic objects which have an obvious connection to space—namely immovable monuments. The locations of historic landmarks, cultural landscapes, or cemeteries are easy to determine, which leads to the fact that preparing of the information system of such landmarks focuses on the development of the structure of the database and method of linking spatial information with descriptive information, or conducting simple analyses of such data.

Usage of information systems of spatial information as applied to the recording of non-material cultural heritage is still in the early stages of development. However, historical GISs represent a very interesting problem, first of all, from the point of view of the conceptual development of the representation of historical phenomena. These phenomena are referenced both chronologically and geographically. This distinction determines how one should capture the element of time in a GIS concept so that map features make the correct interpretation of events possible. Not only the nature of these phenomena or events is of import, but also the range and category of information at hand.

A GIS can prove to be a perfect tool for the accumulation of information and representation of the unfolding of historic battles, skirmishes and other military activities. Interactive maps can render such matters as directions of military offensives, changes in formation arrangements or number of troops not only in a clear and effective way (geographic location complemented by descriptions or illustrations), but also in an attractive manner (animation or multimedia features).

A history-related GIS is of special interest for researchers in the fields of art and material culture. It makes possible the visual representation of contextual and spatial circumstances surrounding cultural heritage phenomena, such as: artists' travels, stylistic influences, import and export of artifacts, scope and character of art patronage, and many others. A spatial information system can be a versatile and easily accessible tool for creating an exhaustive description and analysis of problems related to geographic data.

A spatial information system also can be an effective instrument in presenting the continuous phenomena of non-material cultural heritage. A lack of access to information is the only obstacle in representing how the religious, cultural or ethnic makeup of historic areas changed with time. The ease with which not only qualitative (who), but also numerical information (how many) of an issue in question can be represented in a GIS is crucial. A GIS which processes information on agents of historical changes or migrational routes of human groups in the course of centuries can become an effective research tool in the arsenal of scholars from various liberal disciplines.

REFERENCES

Stanislaw Bialousz et al., "System Baz Danych Przestrzennych dla Wojewodztwa Mazowieckiego," (Warsaw: *Oficyna Wydawnicza Politechniki Warszawskiej*, 2004).

Zaide Duran, Asli Garagon Dogru, Gonul Toz, "Web-based Multimedia GIS for Historical Sites," *International Archives of Photogrammetry, Remote Sensing and Spatial Information Sciences*, vol. 35, part 5, pages 434-437, ISSN:1682-1750

Kazimierz Dynarski et al., "Pismo Swiete Starego i Nowego Testamentu—Biblia Tysiaclecia", *Wydawnictwo Pallottinum 5* (2004).

Ian N. Gregory, *A Place in History: a Guide to Using GIS in Historical Research*, (Oxford: Oxbow; Oakville, CT: David Brown, 2003).

Martyn Jessop, "Promoting Cartographic Heritage via Digital Resources on the Web", *e-Perimetron* 1, no. 3 (Summer 2006) IFCOIHyperlinkhttp://www.e-perimetron.org/Vol_1_3/Jessop.pdf , 246–252.

Alan M. MacEachren, MennoJan Kraak, "Research Challenges in Geovisualization," *Cartography and Geographic Information Science* 28, no. 1 (January, 2001): 3–12.

Lech Ratajski, "Metodyka kartografii spoleczno-gospodarczej," *PPWK* (1989).

UNESCO, "*Convention for the Safeguarding of the Intangible Cultural Heritage.*" (October 17, 2003) http://www.unesco.org/culture/ich/index.php?pg=00006.

Brian A. Zottoli, "Historical Sources in Heritage GIS Mapping: from the Hue Citadel to the Town of Hoi An, Viet Nam,"*Conference on Heritage Management Mapping: GIS and Multimedia. World Heritage in the Digital Age* (October 21–23, 2002): 21–27.

7 Toward Enduring, Global Access to Catholic Research Resources

Ruth Bogan, Diane Maher, Edward D. Starkey, and Jennifer A. Younger

THE IMPORTANCE AND SCHOLARLY SIGNIFICANCE OF CATHOLICISM

The Roman Catholic Church, considered in its broadest sense, is both globally widespread and historically long-lived. There are over a billion Catholics now on earth, almost a sixth of the world's population. Both widespread and ancient, the Roman Catholic Church can also be compared to other major, long-standing civilizations, such as India and China. According to the *Catholic Almanac* this global church is organized into 217,000 parishes divided into 2,667 dioceses, which are themselves members of over 100 conferences. To add to this complexity, there is a second structure comprising religious communities that include monks and nuns, such as the Benedictines and Trappists; friars, like the Franciscans and Dominicans; and dedicated men and women in more recently formed communities, like the Jesuits and the Holy Cross Fathers, as well as many communities of nuns. In addition, the Catholic Church also operates many schools, colleges, universities, hospitals, cooperatives, orphanages and other social service facilities.

We note this complexity not to arrive at some anthropological or political or even religious definition of Catholicism, but rather to consider for a moment the enormous quantity of publications and archival materials which emanate from all levels and dimensions of this church. There are "government publications" from the Church hierarchy and other leadership structures, often taking the form of "letters;" there are newspapers and magazines, both general and local or diocesan; there are minutes of meetings; there are various reports and studies; there are academic monographs and journals; and there is much creative literature inspired by the Catholic religious impulse. In short, Catholic publications of all kinds and in every written language abound along with numerous collections of Catholic archival repositories.

Yet this literature, collected at some level by almost every library on earth, is not really thought of as a single bibliographic entity and seems to lack identification as a "national literature." While acquisitions librarians regularly receive catalogs of "Judaica" or "Americana," catalogs recognized as "Catholica" never cross their desks. Neither is there a central collecting agency for this vast literature. Catholicism has no "national library," no equivalent to the Library of Congress, the British Library or the Bibliotheque Nationale, which have as a primary purpose the collecting of materials reflecting the shared experience of their societies. Even the Vatican Library does not serve this purpose, nor is there any single library or collection of libraries on any continent whose primary function is to collect the overall output of the Catholic experience.

There exists, however, a unique group of institutions in North America that have libraries which purposefully collect parts of the archival and published "Catholica." They are the 230 Catholic colleges and universities in the United States and Canada that are members of the Association of Catholic Colleges and Universities (ACCU). These 230 institutions of higher education range in size from Ph.D.-granting research universities such as Notre Dame, Georgetown, Marquette, and Boston College to small, two-year colleges like Marymount College and Holy Cross College. Fr. Theodore Hesburgh, former president of Notre Dame (1952 to 1987), has often noted that although there are a few Catholic universities in Europe and Latin America as well as a small number in Asia, there is no equivalent collection of Catholic institutions of higher education on any other continent. Notably, we write "collection" of Catholic institutions because these colleges and universities are independent of each other and in no way form a "system." No central authority exists. Nevertheless, these institutions are a unique phenomenon within the Catholic Church. Their libraries and archives may support institutions with broad curricula, often centered on the liberal arts and expanding into professional schools, but they nevertheless often have in-depth holdings of particular areas of church experience. For example, some libraries and archives are affiliated with religious communities which have missions established in foreign countries, leading these collections to often contain photographs, films, newspapers, pamphlets, books, and archival records from these missions.

Although Roman Catholicism can claim a long tradition of self-awareness—the genre of history writing has flourished within it from earliest days—it has nevertheless lacked the dimensions of academic self-study that, for example, have been encompassed in the multidisciplinary field of Jewish Studies for over two centuries now. Professors of Islamic, Buddhist, and Jewish Studies are found in many universities—Harvard was the first university in America to establish a chair in Jewish Studies, the Nathan Littauer Professorship of Hebrew Literature and Philosophy, in 1925—but historically, there have been fewer professors of Catholic Studies. Recently, however, programs of Catholic Studies at Catholic colleges and universities have significantly expanded (Crowe 2002). Among the oldest and best known programs are at St. Thomas University in St. Paul,

Minnesota and John Carroll University in Cleveland, Ohio. Catholic Studies programs are also offered at other pre-eminent Catholic universities, including Georgetown, Notre Dame, St. Louis and Marquette, and new programs are emerging on both Catholic and secular campuses in North America, such as the program at the University of Illinois-Chicago. There are probably more than thirty such programs today. While named chairs for Catholic Studies are not yet as common or as long established as are those for Jewish Studies, with the first chair in Catholic Studies established at Harvard University only in 1958 (Crowe 2002), new chairs too are springing up across the country at Creighton University and secular universities such as Cornell and University of Kentucky. Coupled with this trend is the emerging study of the "Catholic Intellectual Tradition" along with scholarly initiatives to identify elements in the humanities, social sciences and even hard sciences which appear to emanate from the religious culture of Catholicism. This is especially evident in the recent establishment by Fr. James Heft, S.M., of the Institute for Advanced Catholic Studies at the University of Southern California.

THE FORMATION OF THE CATHOLIC RESEARCH RESOURCE ALLIANCE

Eight Catholic university libraries—Boston College, The Catholic University of America, Georgetown, Marquette, Notre Dame, St. Edwards, Seton Hall, and the University of San Diego—founded the Catholic Research Resources Alliance (CRRA) in 2005 to initiate a collaborative effort to share their resources electronically with librarians, archivists, researchers, and scholars interested in the Catholic experience, as well as the general public. In further articulating the proposed initiative, the Steering Committee decided to focus on the needs of researchers and, in the near term, on providing global access to rare, unique or infrequently held research materials in the special collections and archives of Catholic academic institutions and seminaries. While many individuals interested in the Catholic experience will likely find the Portal useful, the Steering Committee identified as the greatest need a mechanism to provide access on a systematic basis to the rare, unique or infrequently held research materials which are essential to today's scholars, yet which are not easily found through other popular means of searching. By electronically bringing together resources dispersed across many collections, the Catholic Research Portal affords the means to discover such resources in print, digital and other formats.

    With the implementation of a working version of the Catholic Research Portal at www.catholicresearch.net, the founding members took the initial step of making several hundred items or collections accessible through the Portal to demonstrate its functionality. Demonstrating a "proof of concept" is an essential element in laying the foundation for expanding both the resources accessible and the number of participating institutions.

From the beginning, questions arose regarding the necessity of a Catholic Research Portal. Searching on the Internet via popular search engines not only retrieves thousands of hits but also requires no special searching knowledge. Yet a comparison of the quality of searching Web-accessible information available through a popular search engine versus searching the archival and library resources discovered through the Portal reveals important differences in items found and relative search productivity.

Searching "Dorothy Day" on the pilot phase of the Portal in its preliminary version finds six hits for manuscript and archival collections of organizations and individuals, all of which are relevant to this subject. While a search through Google Scholar resulted in 114,000 hits, only eighteen of the first fifty (36 percent) are relevant to the subject of this search. While every searcher expects to reject some hits as irrelevant or less relevant, it is quite another thing to have to search through thousands of hits to find those of greatest importance. Furthermore, the hits produced by Google Scholar point only to books or to published articles, while searching done through the Portal results in unique materials relevant to the subject of the search—the papers of important figures and organizations—for which the metadata and finding aids are either dispersed in many different collections, or lacking altogether, or when present are in a print version which is not Web-accessible, or even when in digital format are not fully searchable through popular Internet search engines.

Because of its focus, the Catholic Research Portal will add significant value through the creation of an extensive, highly relevant domain of research resources of and about the Catholic experience. As we saw in the previous search, Google Scholar retrieved millions of hits. Although the most relevant—based on algorithms using keyword frequencies and co-occurrence of keywords—are often displayed first, there are still thousands of irrelevant hits. In contrast, the Portal will provide access to a smaller but highly relevant domain of resources selected from the collections of libraries and archives on the basis of their relevance to those researchers interested in the Catholic intellectual tradition and experience.

In this exciting new digital era, it is easy to think that everything of importance is "on the Web," and indeed we hope that the most significant materials will eventually be digitized, but as pointed out recently in the *New York Times*, not everything can or will be digitized. Hafner (2007) writes about the array of artifacts from John Steinbeck's life and works held at the National Steinbeck Center in Salinas, California:

> The center takes great care to preserve these relics of Steinbeck, a Nobel laureate, yet it has no plans to take the collection a step further, to adapt to a digital age. As a result, the manuscript of "The Pearl" is no more likely to be digitized than is the camper with the

canine-motif curtains that Steinbeck immortalized in his book, "Travels with Charley". . . .

The point here is that these important pieces of history are at risk not of disappearing but of being ignored in the digital age. The author points also to the Library of Congress and states that "despite its continuing and ambitious digitization efforts, perhaps only 10 percent of the 132 million objects held will be digitized in the foreseeable future." If prohibitively high costs are a primary factor here, it certainly will be an even greater obstacle for many smaller collections to overcome. In essence, we fully anticipate that not all collections of unique Catholic records and resources will be digitized in their entirety. Thus, it follows that the creation of global endur- ing electronic access to the metadata of these print resources as well as to digital resources becomes even more of an imperative.

Fortunately, our vision is shared by a number of distinguished leaders drawn from academia, professional associations and the Church. From among these supporters, a Leadership Council has been formed to advise and assist us in promoting the Catholic Research Resources Alliance's vision and mission, both within the Catholic community and the broader community in which we live.

TECHNICAL ASPECTS OF THE
CATHOLIC RESEARCH PORTAL

The central feature of the Catholic Research Portal, and the initial focus of development of the pilot project, was to establish the search interface. Several assumptions or expectations were implicit in our discussions at this early stage of project development. These expectations influenced the sys- tem architecture, the search and display interface for Portal users, the choice of metadata standards, and the development of the administrative module. The early participants expressed a desire to maintain their identities as the owners of and experts about their collections and to be allowed as much control as possible over their descriptive records. In short, they expected the Portal to ultimately direct users to their home sites. From this premise, the developers understood that the portal would collect metadata only, i.e., it would not, at least at first, be a repository of digital objects. In addition, the metadata would need to contain a link to the owning archive.

CRRA members wanted tools to make record submission easy, and they wanted the Portal to reflect ongoing changes and improvements made to their finding aids. This meant that Web-based utilities needed to be devel- oped in which contributors retained some control over their records, allow- ing them to submit revisions as necessary. Although these first contributors to the Portal were well versed in creating sophisticated finding aids, there was consensus that future participants and owners of significant Catholic collections might not have EAD finding aids or any descriptive records at all. Therefore, the development of the Portal needed not only to take into account the level of expertise of the first contributors but also to work toward the inclusion of institutions with less experience in encoding archival finding aids. In response to those expectations, the Portal development team at the University of Notre Dame, with input from the CRRA Metadata and Collection Committees, began to construct a Web-based search interface, a suite of underlying database and indexing tools, and a Web-accessible administrative interface.

FRAMEWORK/INFRASTRUCTURE

The framework for the data storage and search component of the portal employs the modular open source MyLibrary suite with a MySQL database. According to the documentation on its Web site, MyLibrary is "a set of object-oriented Perl modules providing the means for doing input and output against a specifically shaped relations database."[1] MyLibrary incorporates a number of interfaces, which make the data in its database and indexes accessible for various uses: searching, browseable displays, delivery via RSS, and sharing with other metadata repositories via the Open Archives Initiative Protocol for Metadata Harvesting (OAI-PMH). Thus, other metadata portals or repositories will also be able to collect CRRA metadata for display in their systems. The reverse is also true. MyLibrary's database utilizes a structure of fields that are based on Dublin Core metadata elements, making it fairly easy for the CRRA Portal to also collect, index and display metadata from other OAI-compliant repositories.

One characteristic of MyLibrary is its use of a facet and term structure for organizing and presenting data to users. Facets are roughly equivalent to categories, while terms are specific instances of things or concepts within the categories.[2] Facets and terms must be defined by the MyLibrary system implementers. They can be specific to the implementation. They may rely on an established vocabulary like the Library of Congress subject headings, or they may be a combination of both locally defined and external vocabularies. The latter is the case with the CRRA Portal. Currently there are five facets, created by the Portal developers: Formats, Institutions, Names, Subjects and Themes. These terms comprise a mix of vocabularies from various sources. Some terms, like names of Institutions—the names of the archives—are typically encoded in EAD finding aids and can be easily extracted. For the most part, Subjects are Library of Congress subject heading strings, which many of the current CRRA participants use in their EAD finding aids. Formats and Themes are currently defined by the development team and CRRA community. Examples of terms for the Format facet include "Letters," "Directories" and "Clippings." In the first phase of portal development, the Collections Committee defined two Themes:

Catholic Intellectual Life and Catholic Social Action. More recently they identified additional themes, among them Catholic Religious Orders and Catholic Higher Education. As much as possible the terms for the facet/ term pairs will be extracted from fields and elements within the EAD finding aids and bibliographic records. Where the data does not already exist, as is the case with the CRRA-specific Themes, the terms will need to be added to the records.

When XML-encoded finding aids and resource descriptions enter the Portal, specific core data is extracted to the relational database and indexed. The indexer now in use for the CRRA portal infrastructure is KinoSearch, another open source utility.[3] Although KinoSearch provides a search engine, the CRRA Portal developers at Notre Dame opted to create and employ an SRU search client/server utility.[4] SRU (Search/Retrieval via URL) is a protocol used to search Internet databases and indexes. The SRU client sends a query, in the form of a URL with a standard syntax, to the SRU-compliant server. The server deconstructs the URL into its component parts and searches the index. It then returns the results of the query as an SRU XML stream. The client then employs XSLT to convert the search results into HTML for display in the searcher's Web browser.

A query from an SRU client can encode a simple or sophisticated search. For example, a fairly straightforward SRU keyword search against the CRRA Portal for the term "chalice" would look much like this: http:// www.catholicresearch.net/crra/sru/server.cgi?operation=searchRetrieve&v ersion=1.1&query=chalice, where the address of the target server is: (http:// www.catholicresearch.net/crra/sru/server.cgi) followed by the standard SRU instruction to search and return the results of that search (searchRetrieve) for the specified term (chalice).

SRU queries can encode search techniques such as truncation, nesting and Boolean operators and can target specific fields for more precise searching. Built to published standards, the CRRA Portal's SRU interface is easily used. In addition, the use of an SRU interface allows the CRRA portal developers to change the indexer at will—perhaps deciding in the future to exchange KinoSearch for another indexer—without disrupting the search interface.

User Search Interface

Visitors to the Portal will need to search in several ways. Currently the Portal offers a familiar keyword search using a single search box. The keyword search is performed against the full text of all the finding aids and bibliographic descriptions in the database. The Portal also offers an option to browse the collections by the defined facets: Formats, Institutions, Names, Subjects and Themes. These browseable lists allow a user to get a sense of the scope of collections and to view descriptions of an individual resource or a group of related resources without having to generate search terms.

This is an early implementation of the increasingly popular faceted search option on the Web, which guides users to alternately employ keywords and dynamically generated categories of attributes (format, time period, subject matter, location, etc.) to narrow a large result set.

In the initial phase of the project, the text to be indexed and searched arrived in the form of XML-encoded EAD finding aids created by the participating institutions. This presented a challenge to infrastructure developers as finding aids have multiple levels of description, unlike MARC or Dublin Core metadata, which is generally flat. The first phase of portal development achieved a one-dimensional search and display of EAD finding aids that was adequate but disappointing to CRRA participants, who expected that the record display at the CRRA portal would take advantage of the hierarchy of folders and subfolders typical of a full EAD record. After some reworking, the second phase of Portal development has the capability to search both the collection-level descriptions as well as the descriptive text of folders subsumed under the collection descriptions. Folder information displays along with collection level metadata. Future development aims to make clear the relationship of folder level to collection level metadata and to allow searchers to move easily from a specific folder to the full finding aid and from general collection description to the descriptions of individual folders.

Metadata Standards

Another challenge was anticipating where certain critical details had been encoded in EAD records from various sources. Though EAD is an established standard, there are variations in the locations and ways that archivists encode details like unique identifiers or scope notes.[5] During Phase One development EAD records from several of the CRRA contributors were closely examined by members of the Metadata Committee. They subsequently identified, in sample records from participants, the corresponding EAD element or elements where the core data appeared. It was soon evident to the Metadata Committee that the Portal would require minimal metadata standards to ensure that critical data was encoded consistently. The committee, however, questioned how much authority they had to dictate matters of style, content and tagging to the institutions contributing records to the CRRA Portal. As it happened, at the CRRA general meeting in Boston in late 2007, participants not only acknowledged the need for guidelines, but also charged the Metadata Committee to provide them. The charge encompasses core record standards, i.e., required metadata elements, for MARC records as well as EAD finding aids, and requires the Metadata Committee to address controlled vocabularies.

The Metadata Committee was quick to respond and began to draft brief written instructions for contributors. With a number of excellent and extensive best practices documents already written for EAD-based digital libraries, the committee's immediate task was to document those decisions that are specific to the CRRA project. Early in Phase One the committee had identified a core of required metadata based on the Dublin Core and had also included some facet/term combinations in order to take advantage of the MyLibrary structure.[6] Beginning with this set of Dublin Core/MyLibrary elements, which are readily mapped to both EAD and MARC, the Metadata Committee is documenting the CRRA metadata requirements in each of the three standards: Dublin Core, EAD and MARC. Questions about controlled vocabularies arose at the meeting in Boston in 2007, but were not resolved. While Library of Congress subject headings are almost universally accepted by the archives that contributed records in the first phase of development, there was not universal agreement about personal names. One task for the Metadata Committee will be to ensure that, for example, resources about McKenna, Horace Bernard, S.J. do not become separated from resources about McKenna, Horace Bernard, 1899–1982.

Facilitating Data Entry

There are several functional challenges to getting descriptive data into the Portal. The first implementers were able to provide full and often complex EAD finding aids which they simply conveyed to the Notre Dame central site. Future participants will most likely want Web-based data entry forms to input both flat and multi-level descriptions. Portal developers have successfully tested an administrative interface that allows members to input Dublin Core metadata for single resources. Currently a mechanism is also in place, at the administrative Web site, that allows participants to create additional facets and terms. The further development of user-friendly data entry forms is considered a critical tool for helping smaller, but no less important, archives expose their rich resources to Catholic researchers. In the near future we will be testing a Web interface for creating EAD records.

Anticipated Enhancements

In future phases of development, we are planning additional functionality for the Portal. Some desirable enhancements include the ability to export search results to email, files and bibliographic software, as well as more sophisticated sorting options for search results. One consideration, stemming from the assumption that future participants may have limited technological infrastructure of their own, is that the Portal, which currently has a mandate to collocate and index metadata only, may become a repository of electronic finding aids and perhaps even of digital objects for smaller institutions.

FUTURE PLANS OF THE CATHOLIC
RESEARCH RESOURCES ALLIANCE

With over 200 Catholic institutions in North America alone however, a portal that provides enduring global access to Catholic research resources must move from a volunteer effort to a financially supported collaboration with a sustainable administrative infrastructure. This calls for an infusion of funds to leverage the initial investment of the founding members as well as the creation of an organizational structure with the capacity for continuing CRRA's mission.

At the second annual working session, held at Boston College, November 1–2, 2007, members evaluated our progress to date, affirmed ongoing activities and identified future actions. In doing so, we determined that the most pressing issue centers on the need to seek additional funding. While all of the founding members are fully committed to continuing their participation, the lack of project staff such as a project director, a digital archivist and staff with programming expertise, will slow progress to a crawl. Accordingly, several members are developing a three-year plan and budget,and will seek funds from external granting agencies and foundations to provide the project with the necessary staff.

Similarly, we determined that expanding the alliance should rest on a more explicit statement of the activities and responsibilities required of participants, and thus several members will draft a constitution and set of bylaws. The current governance structure consists of the following committees: the Steering Committee, the Collection Committee, the Metadata Committee, the Scholarly Advisory Committee, and the Leadership Council. The Steering Committee, to be renamed the Board of Directors, sets the overall direction, goals and budget. The Collection Committee defines the scope and nature of resources to be made accessible via the Portal. The Metadata Committee establishes the metadata standards, communication protocols and technical infrastructure of the Portal. The Scholarly Advisory Committee will be established to identify the functionality that researchers desire from the portal, while the Leadership Council mentioned earlier assists in promoting the Catholic Research Resources Alliance's vision and mission, and in advising the CRRA on issues of major concern. At this time, the Alliance's governance is self-perpetuating. We recognize, however, the wisdom of bringing new participants into governing roles, and will articulate a participant category with governance responsibilities within the new CRRA bylaws. These bylaws will also provide for a category of sponsors whose primary role is to provide financial and moral support. Fees for all categories of institutional partners—participants, governing members and sponsors—will be a function of the Catholic Research Resources Alliance's financial plan, which is under development and will reflect factors including affordability to participants as well as the need for sustainability.

Plans to Incorporate New Members

The demonstration portal is now operational and the pilot phase is expected to conclude early in 2008. The most obvious next step will be a concentrated effort to expand the number of participating institutions. Early in the project, we created and posted an online directory of directors of Catholic college, university and seminary libraries, archives and library schools so that we could easily communicate with our most immediate colleagues about the project. The libraries, archives and library schools listed are affiliated with institutions that are members of the Association of Catholic Colleges and Universities (ACCU) http://www.accunet.org/ and are located primarily in North America. Already, from among this group, there is a growing list of directors who have over the last two years expressed their strong interest in making their rare and unique resources accessible via the Portal. Such expansion is, however, to a large degree dependent on hiring staff who can provide the direction, training and support for new participants as well as the clarification of participant responsibilities and activities.

Expanding participation just among this group of about 230 institutions is a major undertaking, and to date we have no timeline yet for how rapidly such expansion can take place. Nevertheless, both in anticipation of and independent from this expansion, we have laid out an extraordinarily ambitious set of activities. The first of these is to develop a growth plan to extend the Portal to the collections owned by dioceses, religious orders and additional Catholic libraries in North America. It is widely known that diocesan and religious archives, small as they may be, collectively contain thousands or perhaps millions of rare and unique materials essential to our knowledge of the Catholic experience. The Catholic University of America and the Catholic Library Association hold regular workshops to train these archivists in organizing and describing the materials in their collections, and it is through contact with these workshop participants that we know how keenly interested they are in contributing to the Portal.

To help in developing and implementing the expansion, the Alliance plans to assess the breadth and depth of materials that could be contributed to the Portal by conducting a survey of the ACCU institutions, diocesan and religious archives, and other institutions reputed to have rich holdings in rare, unique or infrequently held Catholic research materials. This survey would ask each institution to identify its most important materials, categorize the extent to which these holdings are rare, unique or infrequently held Catholic research materials, express their level of interest in participating in the Portal, and assess their ability to create metadata records and finding aids. For a similar purpose, the Alliance plans to develop a list of at-risk special and archival collections in Catholic colleges, universities, seminaries, and other Catholic institutions that need early attention for reasons such as inadequate institutional resources for maintaining the collections or harmful environmental conditions requiring immediate action to preserve and retain access to their collections. Then, on the basis of the pilot project, the assessment survey, the list of at-risk collections, and estimates of fixed and variable costs, a plan and budget will be developed to add participants from special collections and archives of small and large institutions to the Portal during a ten-year time period.

We also plan to develop an assessment, timeline and plan for creating access to rare and unique research resources in Central and South America. We are mindful of our responsibilities in the world as it grows ever more connected and fully intend to provide global access to the research resources provided by the Portal. Nevertheless, although certainly a possibility, there are no immediate plans to invite participants from outside of the Americas.

Adding Value to the Research Process

Even though much of the functionality of the Portal rests in its ability to search, browse and analyze the rich metadata in finding aids, the Portal also eventually plans to provide direct access to digital content. Thus, another next step in providing resources for researchers concerns the preparation of a proposal for external funding to digitize selected high priority resources in North America. This digitization project will require that the development of a process and criteria for evaluating and prioritizing digitizable collections of texts, images and artifacts be established.

Another important development to aid researchers involves our plan to develop and implement scholarly services, to go the last mile in ensuring the most support possible is given to researchers when they are evaluating and using the Portal. This service will also entail assessing the need to offer reference services above and beyond the usual services provided to a researcher by the owning institution. Through all of these activities, we recognize that it is vital that there be regular communication with participants, professional and scholarly constituencies, sponsors and other interested parties. We aim to provide scholarly services that put bibliographic data to work for the researcher (e.g., automated text analysis of finding aids to compare similarities of word frequencies to determine document relevancy), to create a space for a virtual researchers community for the exchange ideas and to make possible links that will connect researchers to archival and library experts.

CONCLUSION

While many good things can happen serendipitously, the Catholic Research Resources Alliance has held from the beginning of our conversations an ambitious vision: to create global access to Catholic research resources. No single bibliography exists—not even a single comprehensive listing of what must be thousands of individual archives, libraries and other institutions collecting these resources. Clearly, researchers do find their way to many of these collections, but the creation of a more effective means of discovery has the potential to unleash an outpouring of scholarly productivity—in our own institutions and around the world. Through the collaborative efforts of the Catholic Research Resources Alliance, we are committed to ensuring that these research materials will always be found and accessible to future generations of researchers.

NOTES

1 Eric Lease Morgan et al., *Designing, implementing and maintaining digital library services and collections with MyLibrary*, http://mylibrary.library.nd.edu/documentation/mylibrary-manual.pdf, 123.
2 Ibid., 28.
3 Information about KinoSearch is available at http://www.rectangular.com/kinosearch/.
4 Information about SRU is available at the Library of Congress Web site http://www.loc.gov/standards/sru/.
5 Information about EAD is also available from the Library of Congress at http://www.loc.gov/ead/.
6 Information about the Dublin Core Metadata Initiative is available at http://dublincore.org/.

REFERENCES

Marian Crowe, *The Case for Catholic Studies. Crisis: Politics, Culture & the Church*, September 2, 2002 http://www.crisismagazine.com/september2002/feature5.html|FCC|.
Katie Hafner, "History, Digitized (and Abridged)," *The New York Times*, March 11, 2007 http://query.nytimes.com/gst/fullpage.html?res=9500E5DC1331F932 A25750C0A9619C8B63.

8 Digital Partners
Collaborating to Build Digital Resources

John B. Straw

INTRODUCTION

The advent of digital technology makes new ways of sharing resources possible for the benefit of learning, teaching, and research. The once distinct walls of individual repositories of knowledge are blurring or completely disappearing as libraries, archives, and other historical, cultural, and educational institutions are able to combine resources for virtual access while still maintaining individual ownership.

This concept is not necessarily a rehashing of the buzz about "libraries without walls" that has been around since the words "digital library" were first pronounced. Walls still exist; boundaries are very real and often titanium-strong. Digital technology offers new and expanded doors and windows in those walls, different means of entrance, egress, and travel. It doesn't weaken the load-bearing structures, it adds to their strength through increased access to a larger number of digital resources and through the opportunities provided by digital partnerships.

Identifying potential collaborative opportunities and then developing partnerships to build stronger collections of digital resources has advantages for all the partners, and benefits the clientele of all the institutions involved in the collaboration. To achieve the advantages though, issues such as ownership, copyright, branding, access, costs, and others must be addressed. Written agreements that outline those issues, as well as the goals and each partner's responsibilities, are essential to successful collaborations.

Once partnerships have been established, ongoing communication becomes critical. After collaborative projects have been completed, promoting and publicizing the results of collaboration must include all the partners and their individual and combined clientele. From one collaboration, others will grow if the experience is a positive one and benefits everyone involved.

In exploring the possibilities of digital partnerships, one must assess the positives, potentials, politics, and pitfalls; identify potential partnerships and establish contact; plan and prepare for collaboration; develop the elements of a written agreement; and finally, plan and implement strategies for promoting the use of the results of the digital partnership for the benefit of all participants and their clientele. This chapter examines these elements of digital partnerships, citing examples and experiences from the development of Ball State University's Digital Media Repository, a project of the University Libraries.

POSITIVES OF PARTNERSHIPS

Perhaps the most easily recognized positive effect of digital partnerships is the broader range of materials that can be made available for users. Instead of twenty Civil War letters from one repository, the user will have access to over 100 from three or four repositories, and from a more varied collection of experiences. In addition to photographs of one community in the 1920s, a researcher can study images of life and culture in towns, cities, and rural areas throughout a region. The research experience is expanded exponentially by the increased number of digital resources that can be made available through effective collaboration.

Increased access is another clearly evident advantage of digital partnerships. Collaboration between a county historical society and a larger institution such as a college or university provides a good example. The county historical society operates on a limited budget, is run strictly by volunteers, and is only open for a few hours each week. By partnering with the larger institution to provide access to digital copies of its genealogy materials, the historical society is able to have a world-wide user base through the Internet who might be unable to travel to visit and use the materials during the limited time the society is open for business. Genealogists everywhere will be able to see those family letters on their own time schedule. The county historical society benefits from increased visibility and use. The college or university benefits from the availability of more resources for their students and faculty. Everyone wins.

Some small institutions may be concerned that by providing access to their materials in this manner, their onsite use will decrease. This situation can be a major issue for an institution that depends on the number of visitors to either generate financial support or justify its existence to a board or group of resource allocators. An argument for broader use and a new way of counting usage may be in order.

As budgets fall and costs rise, collaboration on digital projects can be a means to share resources. The partners can share equipment and staff. A smaller institution may only be able to afford a less expensive scanner that allows staff to digitize standard photographs only, while the larger institutional partner can provide equipment for scanning large format items, audio, or video. Equipment can be purchased through a grant and shared with all partners. Pooling resources makes a successful project possible that may not have been financially or practically feasible by any of the partners on their own.

A digital content management system can be a crucial element in the development of successful digital collections. Such a resource provides for control, standardization, searchability, compatibility, and sustainability. Large and effective digital content management systems can be costly. Collaborating with an institution that has a digital management system in place can save money and time. For small institutions, it can be the difference between having a digital presence and not.

In addition to use of a digital management system, other technical considerations can be addressed in a positive way through partnerships. Server space is often an issue that can be resolved through a collaborative arrangement. The necessary technical expertise may be available from one of the partners. Metadata creation requires professional training that may be present at only one of the partner institutions. Compliance with standards also can be achieved through working together.

Finally, a significant positive outcome of collaboration can be success in acquiring funding for digital projects. As mentioned previously, the costs of a digital project can be significant. Sharing costs can be beneficial for everyone. Beyond cost sharing is the increasing need for external funding, particularly through grants. As Deanna Marcum writes, "*Partnership* has become the requisite password for getting any attention from an external funding agency." [1] She points out that grant providers see "the power of digital technology for providing access to information resources, and they know that, through partnerships, even small projects easily can be amplified to bring benefits to many new and often unanticipated audiences."[2] Digital partnerships are obviously an avenue for obtaining external funding in today's competitive financial environment.

POLITICS, PITFALLS, AND PRATFALLS OF PARTNERSHIPS

The numerous positives of partnerships described above may be obvious in most cases. At the same time, the potential problems in developing a collaborative project are often all too clear also. Being aware of and overcoming the politics, pitfalls, and "pratfalls" that may arise in collaborative projects is essential to successful digital partnerships.

The largest elephant in the room most often goes by the name of Ownership, and it is usually accompanied by its cousins, Copyright and Access. For such large creatures, it can be surprising how often we trip over them. These issues should be fully discussed prior to entering into the partnership or beginning the actual collaborative project. They should also be addressed in the written agreement that is developed for the project, as discussed later in this chapter.

The physical objects digitized will remain the property of the partner who owns them. The issues of ownership, copyright, and access pertain more to the digital surrogates that will be created through the collaborative project. How will those digital images be branded? Will they list all partners as joint owners of the digital image? If one institution creates the digital image of the object, it may claim "ownership" of that image. However, the owner of the physical object wants to maintain ownership regardless of format and preserve the right to control copyright and use. One way of handling this issue is to brand the digital object jointly but make clear in the metadata, on the Web page, and elsewhere that all rights remain with the original owner. A statement such as the following that was used for a Library Services and Technology (LSTA) grant project that involved Ball State University Libraries and the Henry County (Indiana) Historical Society, as well as other partners, would be one possibility:

"The historic artifact digitally reproduced in this collection is solely owned and controlled by the Henry County Historical Society, and not by Ball State University. Inquiries about usage, reprint permission, etc. should be directed to the Henry County Historical Society via post at 606 South 14th Street, New Castle, Indiana 47362 or via telephone at (765) 529-4028."

The copyright statement for the digital images in that collection, however, states "Copyright 2008, Henry County Historical Society and Ball State University Libraries. All Rights Reserved." The combination of these two statements is intended to make it clear that while Ball State created the digital image and maintains it in the Ball State University Digital Media Repository, all rights remain with the historical society. Anyone wanting to reproduce or use the digital document in any manner must contact the historical society for permission.

This method may not work in all cases. Citing another example of a digital partnership at Ball State, the University Libraries digitized a local African-American newspaper. The copyright statement for that commercially-produced artifact reads "Copyright 2006, *Muncie Times*. All Rights Reserved." Unlike the partnership with the county historical society, the one with the newspaper was not a grant project. The Ball State University Libraries is simply providing a community service by making the financially-challenged newspaper available online. Every digital partnership will be different and may require different types of statements to satisfy the requirements of each partner.

Making certain that the institution has the right to make digital copies of the materials is essential. The legalities and risks involved in copyright are well known among information professionals. Copyright is a much larger issue than can be adequately addressed here. There are other publications that cover this issue well.

Who will provide and control access, and how that access will be provided, can also be an issue. If a digital content management system is being used, the issue may be moot. Still, access and control issues should be discussed. Information about the image, the size of the image, or even the actual image itself may need to be changed at some point. System requirements may change and have an effect on access to the image. Responsibilities for maintaining access to the images currently and in the future should be agreed upon and clearly stated.

Preservation and security concerns will also arise in putting together digital partnerships. Proper professional handling of archival, original, fragile, unique, and sometimes rare items during the digitization process should be taken seriously. The materials must be kept safe and protected against loss, theft, or misuse. The owner of the original material will insist upon these conditions. Not taking adequate precautions can doom a partnership. The handlers of such materials have an ethical and professional responsibility to care for the items as if they were their own throughout the process. Personnel involved in scanning the items should be well trained and equipped with the proper materials for handling and safeguarding them.

A major obstacle that frequently hampers collaboration on digital projects is the location for scanning items. Most archival repositories, libraries, museums, and other caretakers of historical, cultural, and educational documents and artifacts are reluctant to let their materials leave the premises. If they do not have the equipment, staff, or time to digitize their materials, such projects may never be undertaken. Negotiating where, when, and how items will be digitized as part of a collaborative project is a sensitive and sometimes problematic issue.

A mobile scanning unit is one way to alleviate this problem. For its LSTA grant project working with area repositories to digitize their U. S. Civil War materials, the Ball State University Libraries purchased a mobile scanning unit with grant funds. This unit allowed Ball State personnel and grant project assistants to travel to the county historical societies, public libraries, and museums that were participating in the project to scan their valuable items onsite. The project probably would not have been possible without this unit. The materials were secure and properly handled without leaving the premises. The ability to scan onsite also benefited the project because repository staff members were present to provide valuable information about the items being digitized from their collections.

Not having areas of responsibilities clearly established at the beginning can be a potential pitfall for digital partnerships. The who, what, when, where, and why of a project should be outlined and agreed upon by each partner. Who will do the metadata? Who will do the scanning? When and where will activities take place? Why is a certain part of the project done in a certain way? If the questions are not addressed at the start, there will be stops along the way to get the answers straight, or the questions will surface at the end the project as obstacles to future collaboration. Not having these details worked out can lead to an incomplete, late, or failed collaborative project.

As areas of responsibilities are identified, a big question will often be posed by one or more of the partners: What's in it for me? If the benefits are discussed when the collaboration is first being considered, hopefully that question will have been answered. Unfortunately there are times during a project or even at the conclusion of the project when a partner institution may take a step back and start wondering anew what its institution is really gaining from the effort. Is the return greater than the cost? Most often this type of scenario is "political" in nature. Reiterating the benefits may solve the situation. Sometimes rewording or restructuring the benefits may be necessary.

When questions of responsibilities and benefits occur in a partnership, issues of control may be at the center. Many people have expertise and opinions that can be valuable to a collaborative project. The pitfall happens when the expertise and opinions of individuals become a battle for control instead of a cohesive effort for achievement of the partnership's goals. Finding ways to harness everyone's energy, talents, and contributions instead of competing for control of the processes can be a challenge but will ensure the success of the digital partnership.

While sharing resources (server space, time, personnel, etc.) is one of the benefits of collaboration in developing digital collections, it also can be a pitfall. Determining who contributes what and how much can become another battle for control. Even the largest institution has limits on resources to give towards projects. Balance again becomes important. Each partner institution must honestly assess its ability to provide resources to the partnership. Care should be taken to not fall into the pit of unrealistic expectations or undeliverable promises.

No project will be without politics, pitfalls, and even the occasional pratfall. Preparing for them in advance will make the journey smoother though, and perhaps head off unexpected complications when the collaborative project is complete.

PREPARING FOR PARTNERSHIPS

The first step in developing a digital partnership is determining the possible partners. Factors in the selection process include the project goals, potential users, collections strengths and weaknesses, and subject areas to be covered. For a LSTA project, the Ball State University Libraries decided to create a Digital Repository of U. S. Civil War Resources for East Central Indiana.[3] The goal of the project was larger than just providing digital access to a fairly strong collection of Civil War documents in the Ball State Archives and Special Collections. The purpose was to develop a broad spectrum of materials covering a sizable geographic area, East Central Indiana. Selecting partners from that region who had resources to contribute was the first order of business. Approaching county historical societies, public libraries, and other institutions in the area about their collections of Civil War items, and then holding a meeting of representatives from the institutions to discuss the possibilities, resulted in a workable partnership for the project.

While there may be several potential partners from which to select, keeping the number small will make the project more manageable. More problems can occur when too many partners are involved. For the LSTA grant project described previously, the number of participating institutions was limited to five, even though more were interested. The ones not included in the initial grant project had the opportunity to participate in the project after the grant portion was completed. Even with only five partners, the communication issues, travel arrangements, and the amount of work involved in coordinating all the elements of the project were more difficult than they would have been with fewer participants.

Determining collection strengths and weaknesses is central to selecting the right partners. Examining the areas in your own collection that have gaps or weaknesses will provide guidelines for creating a stronger digital collection that includes materials from partners who have strengths where you are lacking. At the same time, determining areas of strength in your collection will help eliminate possible partners who would perhaps only be duplicating your materials. As stated earlier, one of the main positives of digital partnerships is providing access to a broader range of materials. Selecting partners based on the strengths and weaknesses of collections will help achieve that goal and build a stronger digital collection.

A digital partnership may be based on a particular subject area. Most collaborative digital projects have a particular focus. While a digital collection may be based on type of materials (photograph collection, oral history collection, video collection, etc.), the project focus may be a specific subject area, such World War II, local history, the Great Depression, civil rights, or a myriad of other topics. Repositories that have materials in the focus area of a digital project are the best ones to join in partnerships to create a strong digital collection. Sometimes, though, a repository may only have a few items in the subject area to contribute, but those items are unique or particularly strong examples. In the LSTA grant project for Civil War materials, the United States Vice Presidential Museum in the Dan Quayle Center in Huntington, Indiana, may have seemed like a slightly odd choice for a partner. While the museum did not have the breath of Civil War materials that the other partner institutions had to contribute, it did have unique Civil War documents from U. S. vice-presidents. Having these items in the digital collection gave an added dimension to it.

POTENTIAL PARTNERSHIPS

Digital partnerships can be internal or external to your institution or organization. Internal partnerships can include departments or units of the institution, organizations or groups, and individuals. External partnerships include local community organizations and groups, community members, and local, regional, state, national, or international groups and individuals.

In developing their Digital Media Repository, the Ball State University Libraries established several successful internal and external partnerships.[4] Internal partners include academic departments, students, and faculty:

- College of Architecture and Planning
- Art Department
- Center for Media Design
- Facilities Planning and Management
- Indiana Public Radio
- Indiana Academy for Science, Mathematics, and Humanities
- Ball State Museum of Art
- University Photographic Services
- Physiology and Health Sciences
- Student and faculty artwork
- Theatre Department
- Video Information Services
- WIPB-TV (PBS)

External partners include county historical societies, museums, public libraries, churches, social and service organizations, newspapers, and businesses:

- U. S. Vice Presidential Museum at the Dan Quayle Center
- Delaware County Historical Society
- Henry County Historical Society
- Muncie Public Library
- *The Muncie Times* newspaper

As the digital collections grow, opportunities for new internal and external partnerships occur frequently. Some partnerships are driven by grant opportunities. Others develop through mutual need and desire to provide new resources to support teaching, learning, and research.

The possibilities for digital partnerships are unlimited. They may be put together by institution type, subject, collections, grant funding opportunities, or by a host institution seeking to build stronger digital assets. Whatever the impetus for collaboration or the type of partnership created, developing a written agreement will be crucial for success.

PACTS FOR PARTNERSHIPS

A written contract or letter of agreement is the foundation for any healthy digital partnership. The agreement should:

- Set goals
- Describe each partner's responsibilities
- Identify individuals working on project
- Summarize costs (and cost sharing if appropriate)
- Outline a timeline/calendar
- Include procedures for handling and scanning materials
- Cite standards to be followed.

Special consideration should be given to repository identification and branding. All the partners need to be consulted on how the digital objects will be branded to identify them as belonging to the specific repository, and how the repository will be cited and credited. Nothing can cause more difficulty or even legal complications than not crediting the owner of the original source material. This identification must continue throughout the project and at its conclusion. It should be clearly stated in all publicity as well.

Maintaining communication throughout and following a collaborative digital project is paramount. Contact information should be kept up to date for all partners. Future partnerships may depend on effective communication. Partners should not be forgotten once a project is completed. Additional items may need to be added to a collection, information about the objects or collections might need to added or revised, or some objects may need to be removed at some point. Ongoing communication will ensure that any scenario that may arise can be handled effectively and in a timely manner.

Once the digital project is completed and the resulting digital collection is available for use, some partners may need training and assistance in using the new digital resources. If that is necessary, the partnership pact may include an agreement on who will do the training and how, when, and where it will occur.

PROMOTING PARTNERSHIPS

The ultimate success of any digital partnership is found in the use of the digital resources created and in the response of the users. To ensure that the digital fruits of your labor are sampled by as many people as possible, the results need to be widely publicized to the constituencies of each of the partner institutions. Promoting and publicizing the outcome of a successful project collaboration will also bear fruit for the partners by positioning them as models for other institutions that want to pursue digital partnerships.

Presenting programs at each of the partner sites is an excellent way to reach constituencies. The programs allow for experts to demonstrate how to access and use the digital materials while also affording an opportunity for questions from potential users. They will also provide an opportunity to showcase the repositories where the original materials are kept and inform users about all the other wonderful resources available that have not been digitized yet. An onsite program gives the contributing partner a chance to be recognized for its contribution to the project.

Programs can be part of an opening ceremony for the digital collection. They could also be built around a celebration of some type or an annual meeting. For the LSTA grant project for U. S. Civil War materials, the project director from the Ball State University Libraries was the keynote speaker at the annual meeting of the membership of the Henry County Historical Society, a partner institution. He presented a program on the project and the resulting collection with a focus on the historical society's materials and contributions to the project.

Programs at partner sites will generate local publicity. An article on the program and on the project may appear in the local newspaper. If the partner institution has a newsletter, a story of the program will appear in it, and perhaps a news release will be generated. Depending on the size of the community, there may be a local television or radio station that will do a story. All of these opportunities, in addition to word of mouth among the user community, will generate good visibility and potentially increase use.

Writing a news release, contacting the local media, creating a brochure or poster, and posting the news to Web sites and listserves are all good ways to get the word out. Contacting local schools or other educational, cultural, or historical institutions in the area will be beneficial. Emails can be sent to groups or professional organizations. Explore all opportunities to reach out and make others aware of the results of the digital partnership.

In any publicity that is generated, the roles of each of the partners should be acknowledged. Developing a standard statement to use in any press release or other means of publicity will ensure that no one is left out. Emphasizing the collaborative nature of the project will generate good will and help to secure future partnerships. While all partners should be treated equally in stating their roles in the project, the contribution of one partner may need to be emphasized in any publicity prepared specifically for that partner institution's constituencies. Being "politically sensitive" to the needs of each partner will also foster good will.

In presenting programs and promoting the project, seeking opportunities to expand partnerships should not be neglected. The current project may have had limited partners for various reasons, including helping to keep the project manageable and maintaining everyone's sanity, but a follow-up project to increase the number of digital resources may call for new partners with new resources to contribute. A statement about continuing to build the digital collection created by this project and a call for interested partners may be valuable.

DIGITAL PARTNERSHIPS: THE REASON WHY

Digital partnerships are not necessary. You are probably surprised to see those words in an article that has spent several pages promoting the value of such partnerships and describing the elements of developing successful collaboration, but is had to be stated. Institutions and individuals can conduct successful projects solely on their own. Smaller institutions may not be able to do as much as larger ones, but they may be able to afford a scanner and to put a few images from their collection on the Internet. There are all types of Internet businesses that will help you "do it yourself." So why bother with all the politics, pitfalls, and pratfalls that can come with partnerships?

The answer to that question is our users. Coordinated, collaborative efforts to bring as much of our resources together to provide better access for our users, wherever they may reside, is becoming more critical as a new generation of those users have increased expectations. Someone will provide what those users need and want. Maybe it will be Google, Microsoft, or some other entrepreneurial and opportunistic visionary. Libraries, archives, museums, and other cultural, historical, and educational institutions can either be merely suppliers ("content providers") or they can control their destinies in the new digital world. Digital partnerships provide an opportunity to do the latter.

As Anneke Larrance states, "Leveraging resources is not just about sharing or dividing resources; rather it is the synergistic process of making more from what is available."[5] Digital partnerships allow for leveraging of resources in a synergetic manner, a way to make more for our users. They may provide an opportunity, as Deanna Marcum writes, for "collaboration with partners that have heretofore been strangers."[6] Libraries, archives, and other "stranger" repositories can form "strategic alliances" and use technology to share their unique resources in a new and innovative way for the good of their users.[7]

The results of successful partnerships are worth all the politics, pitfalls, and pratfalls that may be encountered in any collaborative venture. Our users, our customers, are worth it.

NOTES

1. Deanna B. Marcum, "Reconceptualizing Partnerships," in *Virtually Yours: Models for Managing Electronic Resources and Services*, eds. Peggy Johnson and Bonnie MacEwan (Chicago: American Library Association, 1999), 41.
2. Ibid.
3. For more information on the LSTA grant project to create a Digital Repository of U. S. Civil War Resources for East Central Indiana, see *The Library Insider: Ball State University Libraries Newsletter* www.bsu.edu/libraries/virtualpress/libinsider 4, no. 5 (May 2006), 6 and 4 no. 7 (July 2006), 4.
4. For more information on academic, community, and grant digital partnerships of the Ball State University Libraries, see *The Library Insider: Ball State University Libraries Newsletter* www.bsu.edu/libraries/virtualpress/libinsider 3, no. 11 (November 2005), 11; 3, no. 12 (December 2005), 6; and 4, no. 1 (January 2006), 8.
5. Anneke J. Larrance, "Expanding Resources: Benefits to Colleges and University," in *Leveraging Resources Through Partnerships*, eds. Lawrence G.

Dotolo and John B. Noftsinger, Jr. (New Directions for Higher Education, no. 120, Winter 2002), 3.

6. Marcum, 42.
7. John B. Noftsinger, Jr., writes about "strategic alliances" in "Facilitating Economic Development through Strategic Alliances" in *Virtually Yours*, 19–28.

9 Illuminating the Manuscript Leaves
Digitization Promotes Scholarship and Outreach

Rachel I. Howard, Delinda Stephens Buie, and Amy Hanaford Purcell

INTRODUCTION TO MANUSCRIPT LEAVES

Illuminated manuscripts serve as icons for the study of Western European culture from the middle ages to the Renaissance. Since learning in that era typically was associated with the Church, the most common examples are religious in nature, such as Books of Hours and liturgical texts. Similarly the Islamic world has yielded exquisite religious manuscripts, particularly calligraphic copies of the Qur'an and its commentaries, although that culture also has a strong tradition of secular poetry.

Because these older artifacts are written on vellum, in the case of Western European manuscripts, or handmade paper, in the Islamic tradition, many examples have survived through the centuries, and still tend to hold up well to handling and use. Because each specimen is a unique creation, and because they are sought after by private collectors as well as by educators, the more elaborate examples are expensive. They often include minute decorative detail which can be easy to overlook, and impossible to see if an entire class is focused on a single manuscript. Yet illuminated manuscripts provide rich material for study and teaching across multiple disciplines and educational levels. As such, they are good investments for university libraries that have missions to their own institution's faculty and students, as well as to the community beyond.

ACQUISTION AND OUTREACH

At the University of Louisville many people, ideas, and events came together in 2005 to create the Pzena Collection of Illuminated Manuscript Leaves. The University Libraries collaborated with faculty in several disciplines, with a university-community partnership providing outreach to an economically challenged section of the city, and with public school teachers and administrators. Perhaps the greatest single factor, other than the generosity of the Pzena Foundation itself, was the appointment to the University's English faculty of medievalist Andrew J. Rabin. Even before this gifted young scholar moved to Louisville, he was surveying the holdings of the Libraries' rare books collection to make notes of ideas for the classes he was developing and to plan collaborative projects with the Libraries' staff. After his arrival on campus Rabin worked with colleagues to form MEDREN, a regional interest group of scholars working and teaching in Medieval and Renaissance Studies. That same year, the Libraries and the Humanities Division pooled resources to join the Newberry Library's Center for Renaissance Studies. This cooperative association allows the member institutions, forty-six universities from North America and the United Kingdom, to benefit from the Newberry's collections and to develop and participate in joint programs. Through the Newberry, the members also have access to the resources of the consortium of the Folger Institute in Washington, D.C.

Another key element in the equation was Suzy Szasz Palmer, at that time the newly appointed Associate Dean for Collections. Recently arrived from Cornell University, Palmer had been surprised that Louisville's otherwise solid special collections holdings included no examples of Books of Hours. At her urging, Rare Books Curator Delinda Stephens Buie began a search for a specimen appropriate for the Rare Books' budget and collections scope. Six months later she found an early fifteenth-century Book of Hours in Low German, with initials in blue and red. Although lacking the splendor of carpet pages or gold or silver illuminations, the modest volume quickly became a centerpiece for presentations to the K–12 classes visiting the Rare Book Archives.

That year the Libraries also hosted the traveling exhibition on Elizabeth I, funded by the American Library Association (ALA) and the National Endowment for the Humanities (NEH). To augment the handsome ALA/NEH panels, Buie exhibited a selection of thirty sixteenth-century rare books from the University of Louisville collection, and played recorded Elizabethan era music in the gallery. When doing gallery talks, she also brought out the Book of Hours, along with sixteenth-century examples of the university's modest collection of English indentures. The manuscripts proved popular with young students, particularly those in grades 6–8 who had sufficient background in social studies to have some sense of context for the texts. At the same time, while they generally appreciated the centuries-old artifacts and their beautiful letter forms, the students could pretend to be horrified that they were touching animal skins.

As a public university, the University of Louisville collections of rare books, photographic archives, and university archives are, by intention and design, highly accessible. In addition to scholars, publishers, media, and an ever-increasing number of university classes, we encourage use by casual users and visits by community groups. We also find that local and regional teachers, University of Louisville graduates who had visited or worked with special collections during their undergraduate studies, want to bring their own students back. Thus, we regularly welcome K–12 students, whether they are touring campus and the adjoining Speed Art Museum, or coming for an exhibit or program focused on materials from our special collections. Theunissen finds that more libraries are providing such outreach, once the purview of "museums and historical societies," but now part of institutional missions or efforts to be accountable to communities.[1]

During the Elizabeth I exhibition, Libraries Development Officer Traci Simonsen contacted Special Collections with news that the Pzena Foundation had expressed interest in funding an outreach program featuring rare books materials that involved going out into the community to engage at-risk youth. When Simonsen asked Palmer and Buie what would interest this age group, the experience of students viewing the parchment indentures: "Wow, cool!" and "Eeww, gross!" came immediately to mind. We knew that illuminated manuscripts would interest the students if they came to the university to see them. The issue remaining was how—even, whether—to take manuscripts out.

University of Louisville's rare books have traveled before to exhibitions at other institutions and for limited interlibrary loan, both according to ALA's Rare Book and Manuscript Section (RBMS) guidelines.[2] We also have taken small exhibits of literature, popular culture, and local culture out to schools, cultural festivals, and other venues, but we carry along a plexiglass vitrine to cover the materials and limit exposure to light and handling. Certainly school groups come often to Special Collections for exhibits, special programs, and talks by curators. In fact, the Bullitt Collection of Rare Mathematics and Astronomy has long been considered part of the curriculum for an Indiana high school's calculus and advanced placement mathematics classes. In 2005, however, a new principal had limited school trips. For one very special occasion, Buie conferred with university risk management and put her automobile insurance carrier on alert in order to drive four exceptional books to the school: a 1482 first edition of Euclid's *Elementa*, the 1570 first English Euclid with pop-up geometric figures, the 1543 Copernicus' *De Revolutionibus*, and the 1687 first edition of Newton's *Principia* with annotations hand-written by Sir Isaac himself. Class after class, groups of faculty, and an apologetic and grateful principal gathered around each volume in turn, marveling at the importance and proximity of the artifacts.

Although that risky venture out into the community had gone very well, we knew that we could not sustain, promise, or publicize an effort to carry a rare illuminated manuscript volume into schools, even one purchased with private foundation funding. As we considered ways to carry actual artifacts to students without compromising the security and physical integrity of valuable collections, we decided that individual manuscript leaves might be a solution. Such leaves are accessible, affordable, and portable. They allow us to collect a variety of specimens in order to expose students to different genres, texts, and techniques. Individual leaves also offer the possibility that students can respond to the artifacts by creating their own specimens of hand-written, decorated work.

The very real issue standing in opposition to such a seemingly perfect solution was one of curatorial ethics. Book-breaking, the deliberate deconstruction of a book in order to realize a higher profit by selling the leaves as individual lots, is anathema to ethical book and manuscript dealers, rare books curators, scholars, and collectors alike. We approached the ethical issue by conferring with colleagues to establish criteria for purchases. We decided to purchase only those leaves cut from very incomplete fragments of texts and only from texts also readily available in other, complete manuscripts. This limited collecting to established texts of religious works and recognized poets, historians, and authors. Although this ultimately may mean that leaves from the most ephemeral and desirable works, unique vernacular texts, will have no place in the Pzena Collection, the Libraries look forward to eventually making a joint purchase of such a manuscript in collaboration with the Newberry Library.

By 2006 Pzena had made a handsome initial gift, and we asked Professor Rabin to be the Libraries' agent at the annual International Congress on Medieval Studies at Kalamazoo, Michigan. He met with dealers, and made an impressive and diverse selection of leaves: the eighteen specimens included Western European religious texts, Islamic texts, and Persian poetry. An additional gift from the Pzena Foundation will make further purchases possible, allowing us to eventually add examples of Coptic or North African religious texts and European vernacular manuscripts.

COLLABORATING WITH FACULTY
AND GRADUATE STUDENTS

Rabin scheduled a meeting of MEDREN in Rare Books so that regional faculty colleagues could see the new manuscript leaves, consider ways to use them in their own teaching, and contribute ideas for the K–12 project. This session and the ongoing contact that followed were an important part of the collaboration. For example, Rabin and Buie had puzzled over small, regular marks in the margins of a lovely manuscript leaf copied at Citeaux during the period of Bernard of Clairvaux. Another medieval historian immediately recognized the marks as nothing more than hyphens used to justify the margins.

Around the same time, Curatorial Studies Professor John Begley, who was doing preliminary planning for the next semester, asked Buie about the possibility of interesting projects for his graduate students. By the end of their conversation, he had offered his students to design and build the apparatus necessary to safely carry and display the leaves in classrooms, draft lesson plans, and develop interpretive panels which would help prepare K–12 students to see the actual artifacts. Although a great deal of work still lay ahead, many pieces of the complex collaboration had come together.

Rabin, Begley, Buie, and Art History Professor Karen Britt met to consider approaches most likely to engage middle school students. Buie searched the Kentucky Education Reform Act (KERA) curriculum guidelines and found that study of the manuscript leaves could address all areas required by the seventh-grade Arts and Humanities program. At an initial meeting with graduate students, Buie showed the manuscript leaves and the KERA guidelines. Because of his past work as Director of the Louisville Visual Arts Association, Begley already had extensive contact with public school teachers, and was able to invite teachers into the collaboration. The graduate students incorporated the results of the discussion into their own goals for the semester: to develop a sound instructional approach to explain and excite middle school students about manuscript leaves in the University of Louisville rare book collection; to develop a traveling exhibit kit (including pre-visit materials, protective display hardware, and suggested post-visit follow-up activities); to take several (at least three) actual manuscript leaves to students in their classrooms for a viewing and discussion of these fascinating artworks; to encourage teachers and students in inner city schools to do a final project to express their own ideas in words and art on paper, drawing on the examples from the school visits; and to add student artwork inspired by this project to the Pzena Collection as representative artifacts of our time.

The graduate students worked in teams around each of three leaves, representing music, prayer, and poetry, which had been selected for the initial foray into schools. We agreed that another leaf, blank except for rules, would be reproduced and copied for students who preferred to have a template for their own illuminated leaves. The students' collaboration with Buie occurred largely through email and brief individual meetings. This approach required extensive editing and clean up at the finish, but allowed the students more input than might have been allowed in a tightly managed project.

Only one issue escaped consensus. The graduate students demonstrated much more anxiety about the security of the actual leaves in schools, and wanted to keep them within wooden frames and behind glass, while Buie and the public school teachers envisioned more hands-on work with the middle school students. Buie planned to take reasonable precautions; e.g., wearing gloves to hold the original while allowing students to touch with one, very clean, finger, and giving them facsimile copies to freely handle and examine. Theunissen suggests that such issues stem from the different orientations of librarians and museum curators:

> Unlike museums, which display their collections under glass in a protective environment with uniformed guards, rare book collections have traditionally permitted, with a few exceptions, a gloved, hands-on approach. Achieving a balance between preservation and access is an ongoing issue for special collections regardless of the educational

background of the user. However, when a group of ten-year-olds is gathered around a table to view several volumes printed in the fifteenth century, the preservation factor becomes critical. By placing the rare book, opened to an illustration, towards the middle of the table and setting a facsimile volume in front of it, a compromise is struck. Young hands can explore the surrogate copy with minimal hovering by staff and hopefully the excitement of seeing a 500 year old book is not diminished.[3]

Coming from a library special collections background, and a firm believer in that balance between preservation and access, Buie knew if any one of these leaves began to show signs of wear, it could, if necessary, be removed from classroom use and replaced with a leaf of a comparable genre and quality. This level of comfort could secure the opportunity for at-risk students to touch the vellum, see light shine through the marginal prickings, and feel the texture of gold on gesso. The experience might help them better understand the process of creating a manuscript, or imagine the life and work of a French monk or Persian calligrapher.

The Curatorial Studies students' work resulted in a polished, professional looking presentation for the artifacts. Begley reproduced the students' introductory panels in glossy color and mounted them on foam core, in addition to laminating facsimiles of the leaves with teaching points on the back of each. One graduate student offered to go to middle schools and help with transportation, security and teaching. Another student, a musician as well as an aspiring museum curator, found a modern transcript of the antiphonal text, and provided a recording of his own voice chanting the music.

The contributions of scholars such as Rabin and Begley cannot be over-emphasized. Katz, himself a scholar, suggests " . . . the greatest failure of scholarly libraries in my lifetime is that they have not enlisted the active participation of scholars in planning, administration, and decision-making. Correspondingly, the greatest failure of the scholarly community has been its failure to engage the libraries and the librarians."[4] Katz continues by mentioning the new pedagogical emphasis on " . . . the combination of the availability of source materials in digital forms and the focus on active learning based on real-life experimentation with research data. This emerging conjunction provides an entirely new environment in which there is no longer a distinction between scholarship and teaching. And special collections are likely to be one of the crucial sites for this process to take place."[4] For now in the academic environment, at least in the humanities where the scholarly monograph remains the gold standard for the award of tenure, such collaborations have little tangible reward to offer a young professor beyond an entry under "service" on the *curriculum vitae* and the acknowledgement of those of us grateful for their expertise.

Another major collaborator arrived on campus in August 2006: Rachel Howard, the University Libraries' first Digital Initiatives Librarian. In preparation for her coming, Associate Curator for Special Collections Amy Hanaford Purcell had organized the purchase of the Libraries' first high-end overhead scanner. Although Terry Abraham writes of scanning photographs during his lunch time on a borrowed scanner, our higher resolution, more intentional approach would eventually meet the necessary requirements for images destined for viewing via JPEG2000.[5] In fact, Howard and Purcell used the manuscript leaves as tests for the new equipment, and Howard decided to include a project based on the Pzena Collection within the Libraries' CONTENTdm-based Digital Collections, which launched in 2007. This digital presentation will allow teachers and students on-going access, broaden their study of the manuscript leaves beyond in-class presentation of the artifacts, and enable scholars in MEDREN and at great distances to extend their analysis and discussion of the manuscript leaves. In turn, the Libraries will continue to refine the digital project as the scholars study details, make new discoveries, and contribute their work to the project.

The decision to provide online access to the manuscript leaves complicated the collaboration even as it augmented it. Abraham celebrates digital approaches: "In online formats, electronic data is easy to update, it is stored in a compressed format until accessed, distribution is solely to those who want the information, and the costs of publication, distribution, and storage are, in some environments, almost nil."[6] Traister, on the other hand, recommends careful consideration of the implications of such projects, including the significant costs of staff time, stress and strain on materials, equipment, and space. "Librarians and faculty both need to give such projects considerable thought—and calculation in a literally arithmetical sense—before anyone embarks on them."[7] Probably, however, many institutions will agree with the University of Louisville Libraries that it is necessary to do a project at least once before it is possible to measure the inputs. Even then, the demands of another project, based on different formats and with different contributors or purposes, will vary.

DIGITIZING THE MANUSCRIPT LEAVES

In its digital initiatives, the University of Louisville Libraries attempts to follow the framework established by the National Information Standards Organization (NISO) in *A Framework of Guidance for Building Good Digital Collections*.[8] The second edition of this document, published in 2004, builds on an earlier version developed with funding from the Institute for Museum and Library Services (IMLS) with the intention of "encourag[ing] institutions to plan their digitization practices strategically in order to develop collections that will be accessible and useful for the long-term, and that can integrate with other digital collections to support a growing network of broadly accessible digital information resources."[9] Some of the *Framework*'s recommendations are accommodated by the software used for indexing and access (in our case, CONTENTdm digital media management software). Others must be built into the policies and practices of the institution. This section will outline our general procedures as they relate to the *Framework*, using the *Illuminating the Manuscript Leaves* digital collection as a case study.

The *Framework* begins by stipulating that "a good digital collection is created according to an explicit collection development policy that has been agreed upon and documented before digitization begins."[10] At the University of Louisville, we have collection curators fill out a Digital Project Proposal which asks for details about the size and scope of the project and the status of the materials in terms of processing, preservation, cataloging, and copyright. Determining the size and scope of a project can be more difficult than it sounds: if a collection has not been fully processed, the curator must thus take responsibility for organizing the collection to the point where its size can be defined, since that has bearing on how to allocate resources for scanning and cataloging. If the scope of a digital collection does not match the scope of the physical collection, that needs to be explained and justified so that subjective decisions about what to digitize do not erode the context of the original materials. Copyright issues should be addressed up front, as they may derail a digital project or entail additional work to secure the appropriate permissions to proceed.

Fortunately, the date of the manuscript leaves' creation placed them squarely in the public domain, and the size and scope of the collection were similarly simple to determine: the eighteen leaves selected and purchased in 2006 would form the digital collection. The manuscript leaves were in excellent condition and had already been rehoused in archival boxes and assigned item-level numbers, rendering additional processing and preservation treatment unnecessary. The status of the cataloging, however, loomed largest as a resource need: very little information accompanied the manuscript leaves, and it would need to be verified, expanded, and formatted to our metadata standards in order to be searchable online and to make the materials useful to teachers. Indeed, the metadata required more time than any other aspect of this project.

We also ask for an evaluation, on the scale of one to five, of the access, preservation, and other needs or opportunities enhanced or presented by the creation of digital surrogates and standardized information about them. This aspect of the digital collection development policy enables us to prioritize among the many possible digital collections, and to articulate those decisions to stakeholders such as administrators and funders, as well as in publicity materials. While the impetus for selecting manuscript leaves for digitization included a desire for increased access to them, the *Illuminating the Manuscript Leaves* project rated especially high on "opportunity" factors: it ties in to a university-wide strategic initiative (working with underprivileged youth in the community); involves partnering with educators and students to create lesson plans relating to these historically and culturally important materials; and adds functionality to the study of the material by creating high-quality digital files that allow for image and textual analysis. Even the decision to use a descriptive title for this digital project rather than a straightforward collection name reflects our vision of it as being more than merely a digital surrogate for a physical collection.

After approving a digital project proposal, we plan the approach to digitization. In this case, we began by determining formats for the digital files. As a general rule, we scan images as uncompressed TIFF (Tagged Image File Format) files in 24-bit RGB color, at a minimum resolution of 600 pixels per inch (ppi), with a spatial resolution large enough to allow for the creation of 8 x 10 inch prints directly from the TIFFs. As described in the U.S. National Archives and Records Administration (NARA)'s Technical Guidelines for Digitizing Archival Materials for Electronic Access: Creation of Production Master Files—Raster Images, master digital files should serve as a "reasonable reproduction" of the physical items at the time of scanning (rather than using technology to repair imperfections in the original), and should be done in a "use-neutral" manner, not for a specific output.[11] The Framework concurs with this approach: "A good object is digitized in a format that supports intended current and likely future use or that supports the derivation of access copies that support those uses. Consequently, a good object is exchangeable across platforms, broadly accessible, and will either be digitized according to a recognized standard or best practice or deviate from standards and practices only for well documented reasons."[12]

In other words, we strive to create a high quality master digital file that replicates the physical object's appearance, and we use that master file to create other "service" files for specific purposes (to display on screen, to print, to enlarge and highlight a detail on screen or in print, etc.). Because of the rich detail (both imagery and text) in the manuscript leaves, we decided to scan the TIFF files at a resolution of 1000 ppi rather than the usual 600 ppi. Purcell scanned each side of each leaf using the BetterLight overhead scanning setup, because the leaves typically exceed the scan area of a standard flatbed scanner. She assigned file names to the digital files concluding with "r" for recto and "v" for verso, although later we realized that the Persian and Arabic texts would actually have been read from right to left, meaning that the file labeled "v" actually belonged before "r." This issue was resolved at the time of metadata entry, but highlights the importance of having subject specialists involved at various stages of digital projects, because such seemingly minor matters can have an affect on the quality of the end product. Such issues also underscore the necessity of documenting all decisions, including brief notes on rationale.

Anticipating the need to examine details of imagery and text, we decided to create service copies in JPEG2000 format, which uses wavelet compression to reduce file size while enabling zooming and panning of the image.[13] Our CONTENTdm license includes two JPEG2000 acquisition stations, from which JPEG2000 files can be created from TIFF master files. (Once created, JPEG2000 files do not require a separate plug-in for access.) Because CONTENTdm manages both the digital media and the information about it (metadata), and because the people with the expertise to create the metadata were not comfortable learning how to use the software, preferring instead to document their research in word processing and database systems with which they were already familiar, we postponed the conversion of the TIFFs to JPEG2000s until after the metadata had been prepared and was ready to be ingested along with the TIFFs into CONTENTdm.

Metadata is truly the axis around which all other elements of a digital collection orbit. Its centrality to the digitization workflow cannot be overstated. The Framework asserts, "A good object will have associated metadata," and goes on to delineate six principles of good metadata, or information related to the object, including its need to support interoperability, rights management, and long-term management; the use of standards and vocabularies; and its appropriateness to "the materials in the collection, users of the collection, and intended, current and likely use of the digital object."[14]

A local team of experts had already constructed a data dictionary for the University of Louisville Digital Collections, based on the Dublin Core Metadata Initiative (DCMI) Element Set (used by CONTENTdm), the Collaborative Digitization Project's "Dublin Core Metadata Best Practices," and the University of Washington Libraries Metadata Implementation Group's "Metadata Guidelines for Collections using CONTENTdm."[15, 16, 17, 18] In order to accommodate these particular materials and the target audience of users, we revisited and modified some of the fields for the manuscript leaves metadata. Significantly, we added fields for both the language and the script of the manuscripts' text, as well as a description of the ornamentation style, and we adapted the "Location Depicted" field (mapped to the Dublin Core "Coverage" element and used to refer to the location at which a photograph was taken) to "Place Original" (also mapped to "Coverage" but representing the location at which the manuscript originated).

Armed with the framework of the data dictionary, subject experts worked together and with local metadata experts to research and format information about each manuscript leaf. This proved to be the most time-consuming aspect of the project because of the myriad details requiring research, from identifying an unfamiliar script to determining the current standardized name of an Ottoman Empire location to distinguishing an author (who composed a text) from a scribe (who rendered a particular manifestation of it) to, as mentioned above, determining the direction in which text should be read in Western and Eastern cultures. Once complete, the metadata could be united with the JPEG2000 version of the manuscript in CONTENTdm.

TEACHING WITH MANUSCRIPT LEAVES

Shortly before the launch of the digital collection, we had an opportunity to show the manuscripts to a group of at-risk students from a middle school in an economically disadvantaged section of the city. The students were visiting campus under the auspices of the University of Louisville's Signature Partnership. This broad and ambitious program, initiated with community partners including Louisville Metro Government, Jefferson County Public Schools, Metro United Way, Louisville Urban League, and faith-based institutions, seeks to reduce social and human disparities in education and other areas such as health and economic development. The program coordinates multi-disciplinary academic, research and service activities of the university towards meeting critical needs of the community. One of the first projects was to bring at-risk students to campus to make them feel comfortable and welcome, and to inspire individual visions of attending university one day. We wanted to bring students to the library and decided that the illuminated manuscripts would be a key feature of the agenda.

Purcell organized the effort to gather over 100 middle school students for a presentation that included former University of Louisville basketball great and community hero and leader, Darrel Griffith, and one of Special Collections' Federal Work Study Program students, education major JoAnna Cruz, who described herself as a former at-risk student. Both Griffon and Cruz spoke with passion about education, research, and the treasures awaiting the students in the Libraries. The key link to the manuscripts themselves, however, was the presentation of English professor Andrew Rabin.

Since the digital project was not yet available online, Purcell had worked with Rabin to select some of the scanned manuscripts for display in PowerPoint, so that the images could be displayed on huge screens behind him as he spoke. Although the exquisite images captured the attention and enthusiasm of all adults present, Purcell noted that the students themselves remained polite, but looked bored until Rabin began to speak. Rabin sometimes jokes about appearing in pelts and Viking horns to enliven his students, but his dynamic presentation, even without such accoutrements, turned the static images into a powerful attraction, securing the students' imaginations and drawing them into the historic documents. As envisioned at the beginning of the project, the students were most interested by the Rabin's graphic—"Eeww, gross"—account of vellum making. Once their middle school veneer of cool was disrupted, the youths joined the adults in appreciation of the leaves.

This experience taught us that the best material, delivered through the most effective visual presentation, still requires personal interpretation and skilled presentation. We realized that this would be true in middle school classrooms, and in the presentation of the manuscript leaves as a digital collection. Abraham notes: "The popular saying is that a picture is worth a thousand words; in our experience a picture requires a thousand words to tell you what you are looking at."[19] Although the inclusion of metadata and links helped Buie achieve a long-held desire to do a digital version of the eighteenth- and nineteenth-century practice of extra illustration, it proved particularly challenging to strike a balance between the detailed explanatory material likely to be useful for scholars and the broad descriptions more accessible to middle school students.

LAUNCHING THE DIGITAL COLLECTIONS

Meanwhile, the Libraries' Head of Web Resources, Terri Holtze, worked with Buie and Howard to create a home page for the *Illuminating the Manuscript Leaves* digital collection.[20] Holtze built links to CONTENTdm's search and browse functions for this collection, and chose and coded the colors, layout, and Flash display to make the Web site an attractive and enticing destination, as recommended in the Framework: "A good collection-building project has a substantial design and planning component."[21]

Howard and Buie prepared essays to provide context, navigation assistance, and lesson plans. In keeping with the *Framework*'s principle of describing collections so that a user can discover its important characteristics, we include an About the Collection essay with every digital collection, including a scope and content note, a conditions of use statement, and an acknowledgments section delineating the people, equipment, and standards used to create the digital files, metadata, and other interpretive material associated with the online presentation.[22] In order for this record to be complete, we must have good documentation of each step in a collection's acquisition, processing, and digitization. This is not always the case, but our hope as we move forward is to better track our workflow for our own sake as well as for the sake of the user. Fortunately, the task of writing about the manuscript leaves collection was simple, due to its recent acquisition, lack of copyright complications (all items are in the public domain), and rapid flow through the various stages of processing, scanning, and description.[23]

The Web site also incorporates the work of the Curatorial Studies students, with a detailed statement and citations of how the project addresses KERA core content goals for the seventh grade Arts and Humanities program.[24] Individual pages for the three leaves used by Curatorial Studies students include key points and links to additional information.

Once all the pieces (scans and metadata integrated into CONTENTdm; essays and design prepared in HTML) had been assembled, we reviewed the presentation for accuracy and completeness, then made the URL available to the public in August 2007. Reaction has been positive so far, although we have not yet formally analyzed usage statistics, nor have we conducted an assessment of the Web site. We intend to do so in the future, and to disseminate that information broadly.[25]

All contributors to the literature agree that a Web presence amplifies the demand for reference and access instead of serving merely as a surrogate. Abraham points out that although geographical barriers to use of special collections diminish in an online environment, they do not entirely disappear. " . . . it is unlikely that digital surrogates of 'everything' can be placed on the Web, in spite of those requesting and expecting it." Nevertheless, researchers can be "better prepared for having accomplished a certain amount of preliminary work through Web-based resources before arriving."[26]

The University of Louisville Libraries' first significant Web-based presentation, a 2001 catalog of a selection of the Libraries special collections *For Love of Learning*, brought reference requests and visitors from around the globe.[27] The project created a demand for more access, and for more digital availability. Visser finds "In the special collections at CU-Boulder, we still have patrons for whom it is inconceivable that not all of our materials have online records and that not all of our manuscripts have been digitized and made available online. These expectations of the electronic sphere are also permeating the rest of our culture. People expect to have access to information and materials, they expect to have it now, and they expect (rightly so) for it to be packaged or presented in an accessible way for those with special needs."[28]

Similarly, contributors to the literature find Web presentation particularly helpful for introductions to materials and topics essential to a successful special collections experience. Schmiesing and Hollis stress its advantages: " . . . providing background information before the visit through an introductory lecture in the classroom, a worksheet, or notes posted on the Web ensures that students receive as much time as possible to view the materials during their visit."[29]

NEXT STEPS

The next phase of the project, taking the manuscript leaves into classrooms, lies ahead. Three middle schools with at-risk student populations have invited us: the school involved in the aforementioned Signature Partnership, a school several blocks from the university campus, and a school recruited when the principal invited Buie to discuss creation of a school archive. Working with the social studies coordinators at each school, we have alerted faculty to the Digital Collections site and invited critique of the lesson plans there. As the sessions in schools are scheduled, the panels and introductory materials created by the Curatorial Studies students will go out to schools two weeks before the curator takes the leaves into schools. Although the lesson plans currently encompass only three of the leaves, Schmiesing and Hollis' point: "Students are further engaged when they are involved in deciding which materials will be on display and which themes and topics they may wish to investigate while viewing the materials," is valuable.[30] The three leaves will travel to every classroom, but we also will invite the middle school students and teachers to request one or two additional leaves from the selection on the Web site.

The *Illuminating the Manuscript Leaves* Web presentation will grow and change, with works created by middle school students; additional Rare Books manuscript holdings; and feedback from scholars anticipated. We must also establish a system for students and teachers to evaluate the program. Visser points out that special collections departments " . . . are in a position to create an understanding of the importance of unique or rare materials, to inspire a sense of awe when confronted with a tangible, historical object, and to acquire an appreciation of how digital imaging and the electronic world are creating exciting possibilities for special collections materials."[31] Pedagogical principles, as well as common sense, require that we determine whether these goals, and the goals attending the gift of the Pzena Foundation, are realized.

NOTES

1. Yolanda Theunissen, "Developing and Promoting Outreach Services for Elementary and Middle Schools: Case Study of a Rare Map Library at a Public University," *Journal of Map & Geography Libraries* 3, no. 2 (June 2007): 11.
2. ACRL-RBMS, *Guidelines for Borrowing and Lending Special Collections Materials for Exhibition*, January 2005, http://www.ala.org/ala/acrl/acrl-standards/borrowguide.cfm (September 10, 2007).
3. Theunissen, 15.
4. Stanley N. Katz, "Scholars and Teachers: Hidden Partners for Hidden Collections," *RBM: A Journal of Rare Books, Manuscripts, and Cultural Heritage* 5, no. 2 (Fall 2004): 120.
5. Terry Abraham, "Unlocking the Door to Special Collections: Using the Web Combination," *Library Philosophy and Practice* 3, no. 2 (Spring 2001): p. 36, http://www.webpages.uidaho.edu/~mbolin/abraham.html (September 10, 2007).
6. Abraham, par. 33.
7. Daniel Traister, "Public Services and Outreach in Rare Book, Manuscript, and Special Collections Libraries," *Library Trends* 52, no. 1 (Summer 2003): 93.
8. NISO Framework Advisory Group, *A Framework of Guidance for Building Good Digital Collections*, 2nd ed. (2004) http://www.niso.org/framework/Framework2.pdf (September 10, 2007).
9. Ibid., iv.
10. Ibid., 3.
11. Steven Puglia, Jeffrey Reed, and Erin Rhodes, *Technical Guidelines for Digitizing Archival Materials for Electronic Access: Creation of Production*

Master Files–Raster Images, 2004 http://www.archives.gov/research/arc/digitizing-archival-materials.pdf (September 10, 2007).

12. NISO Framework Advisory Group, 14.
13. Joint Photographic Experts Group, "JPEG2000: Our New Standard!"http://www.jpeg.org/jpeg2000/index.html (September 10, 2007).
14. NISO Framework Advisory Group, 19–29.
15. University of Louisville Libraries, *CONTENTdm Cookbook: Recipes for Metadata Entry for UofL Digital Initiatives*, August 2007 http://digital.library.louisville.edu/cdm4/cookbook.pdf (September 10, 2007).
16. Dublin Core Metadata Initiative (DCMI), *Dublin Core Metadata Element Set, Version 1.1*, December 2006 http://dublincore.org/documents/dces/ (September 10, 2007).
17. CDP Metadata Working Group, *Dublin Core Metadata Best Practices, Version 2.1.1*, September 2006 http://www.cdpheritage.org/cdp/documents/cdpdcmbp.pdf (September 10, 2007).
18. UW Libraries Metadata Implementation Group, *Metadata Guidelines for Collections using CONTENTdm*, June 2004 http://www.lib.washington.edu/msd/mig/advice/default.html (September 10, 2007).
19. Abraham, par. 37.
20. University of Louisville Rare Books, *Illuminating the Manuscript Leaves*, August 2007 http://digital.library.louisville.edu/collections/mss (September 10, 2007).
21. NISO Framework Advisory Group, 30.
22. Ibid., 4.
23. University of Louisville Rare Books, "About This Collection," *Illuminating the Manuscript Leaves* http://digital.library.louisville.edu/collections/mss/about.php (September 10, 2007).
24. University of Louisville Rare Books, "Illuminating the Manuscript Leaves: Lesson Plans," *Illuminating the Manuscript Leaves* http://digital.library.louisville.edu/collections/mss/lesson.php (September 10, 2007).
25. NISO Framework Advisory Group, 9, 31–32.
26. Abraham, par. 43.
27. University of Louisville Libraries, *For Love of Learning: an Introduction to Special Collections & Primary Sources at the University of Louisville Libraries and Archives*, 2001 http://special.library.louisville.edu/index.stm (September 10, 2007).
28. Michelle Visser, "Special Collections at ARL Libraries and K–12 Outreach: Current Trends." *Journal of Academic Librarianship* 32 (2006): 317.
29. Ann Schmiesing and Deborah R. Hollis, "The Role of Special Collections Departments in Humanities Undergraduate and Graduate Teaching: A Case Study," *portal: Libraries and the Academy* 2, no. 3 (April 2002): 474.
30. Schmiesing and Hollis, 473.
31. Visser, 319.

10 I See the Light

Using Web-based Exhibits to Enhance Interactive Archival Scholarship

Suzan A. Alteri and Daniel D. Golodner

INTRODUCTION

All societies look inward in order to learn and mold their perceptions of the collected past. It is the archivist's responsibility not only to be the curator of our past, but also to be the courier of its content. The challenge to all archives and libraries, including those dealing with social history, is to present the past in a way that accurately conveys historical events, while at the same time taking advantage of the newest technologies to reach a larger audience.

In an article earlier this year, Katie Hafner of the *New York Times* documented how history could potentially disappear in the digital age.[1] She noted that increasingly a growing generation of researchers prefers primary source material—the backbone of an archive—to be in electronic format, easily at their fingertips. This dependence on electronic information gathering has created a quandary for archives and academic institutions. Traditional archivists lament that this could be the death of the archive, with users preferring to use a computer rather than coming to a physical space and consulting paper documents. Their fears appear to be unwarranted given the fact that online research often encourages scholars to visit archives in the hope of discovering more source material. This change in information gathering is transforming the way scholars perform research, and indeed, it is changing scholarship itself. Thus, archivists and librarians need to look ahead to future trends of information science and think along less traditional means of access and communication in order to remain relevant.

Emerging technologies such as social networking and Web 2.0 offer archivists and librarians the ability to enhance research needs and even affect research trends. Aware of these new possibilities, the Walter P. Reuther Library decided to revamp a virtual exhibit of one of its most popular research collections—the 1968 Memphis Sanitation Workers Strike. These materials are part of the collection of the American Federation of State, Municipal and County Employees (hereafter AFSCME).

This new exhibit allows users to comment and share information, thus encouraging a dialogue among researchers, students, and archivists. It changes the way research is done in real time by providing scholars with documents they previously only could obtain through a laborious trip to the archive or through lengthy conversations with a reference archivist. This chapter outlines the project parameters, the creation of the new exhibit, beta-testing, and the potential benefits for technical service archivists. It also discusses the advantages and potential pitfalls of interactive Web-based messaging tools.

SCHOLARS AND THE HISTORY OF THE
MEMPHIS SANITATION STRIKE

The Memphis Sanitation Workers Strike was a watershed event in American history. It united members of the labor and civil rights movements, community organizers, church activists, and student protesters, and had a lasting impact on unionism in the South. It began on February 12, 1968 when 1,300 African-American sanitation workers walked off the job due to discrimination, poor working conditions, lack of safety and job protection, discrepancies in pay between themselves and white sanitation workers, and the lack of vacation and sick leave. At the time, forty percent of African-American sanitation workers could qualify for welfare at the wage they received from the city. Many worked two to three jobs to feed their families. African-American workers were sent home and not paid during poor weather while their white counterparts stayed at the workplace and were paid. While white workers were given new trucks, the African-American workers were forced to use broken down trucks, and lift heavy garbage cans that often covered them with maggots and rotten food. Above all, these workers were supposed to be grateful for their jobs and were not expected to complain about lack of safety or workman's compensation.

Prior to the walkout, T.O. Jones, who later became the leader of Local 1733, quietly organized workers into a local under the auspices of the AFSCME. It was difficult at first, but after two African-American sanitation workers were killed seeking shelter from a sudden storm in the back of the truck, the men had finally had enough and walked out. While the major papers of Memphis and the white majority living in the city supported the mayor's refusal to negotiate with the workers, the Memphis AFL-CIO and the powerful Shelby Democratic Club stood by the strikers. It wasn't long before local churches became involved in an effort to quell rising tensions. Eventually, the black community would join in the efforts to aid the strikers through a series of marches, vigils, gospel singing, and donations of clothes, food, and money. This marked the first time that organized labor, civil rights workers, church activists, community organizers, and student protesters merged to form a movement called COME—Community on the Move for Equality. Reverend Lawson, a prominent African-American clergyman with ties to Martin Luther King, Jr., headed up the strategic planning committee for the strike, which included daily marches, particularly after the fateful violent march that took place on March twenty-third. During these daily marches the strikers simply wore signs that stated: "I AM A Man."

Almost every American knows that Dr. Martin Luther King, Jr. was shot in Memphis, but few know why he was really there. King had come (first in late March and then again in early April) at the behest of Reverend Lawson, who feared growing tensions and violence in Memphis, to support the sanitation workers and to prove that one could lead a successful nonviolent strike. But King did not simply arrive to prove his nonviolent theories. The struggles of the civil rights movement had also galvanized King to fight for broader economic and social justice. He wanted to build bridges between the labor movement and the civil rights movement, but he also wanted to aid those who were at the bottom of the ladder.

> Memphis Negroes are almost entirely a working people. Our needs are identical with labor's needs—decent wages, fair working conditions, livable housing, old age security, health and welfare measures, conditions in which families can grow, have education for their children and respect in the community. That is why Negroes support labor's demands and fight laws which curb labor. That is why the labor-hater and labor-baiter is virtually always a twin-headed creature spewing anti-Negro epithets from one mouth and anti-labor propaganda from the other mouth.[2]

This is an excerpt from Martin Luther King, Jr.'s last speech, "I've Been to the Mountaintop". On April 4, 1968 he was assassinated outside his hotel room at the Lorraine Motel.

Scholars have gravitated towards this pivotal event in modern American history. Michael K. Honey has written three books on the strike, *Southern Labor and Black Civil Rights, Black Workers Remember: An Oral History of Segregation, Unionism, and the Freedom Struggle,* and most recently, *Going down Jericho Road.* Joan Turner Beifuss deftly chronicles the strike in *At the River I Stand,* while Taylor Branch and David J. Garrow have placed the events of the strike in the larger context of the civil rights movement. While many works deal with the assassination of Martin Luther King, Jr., others have focused on the cooperation during the strike of the labor movement and the civil rights movement.

There are a large number of research topics available to scholars and researchers, and high school students looking for topics during Black History Month. The trouble, however, for these researchers is that the primary source materials are scattered across various collections within the larger organizational collection of AFSCME, thus forcing scholars and archivists to hunt through boxes for crucial documentation of the strike and its aftermath. Moreover, documents also reside at the Mississippi Valley Collection at the University of Memphis, making the process of scholarly documentation a painstaking and costly process. In the digital age, however, research does not have to be so difficult. The archive can digitize necessary documents to save time for both scholar and archivist and place them on the Web. Thus, virtual online exhibits can both educate and serve as a reference tool.

THE 2003 ONLINE EXHIBIT: CREATION AND EVALUATION

The original exhibit in the Walter P. Reuther Library opened in 2003 to celebrate the thirty-fifth anniversary of the strike. The exhibit itself took four months to prepare, and the intention was to turn the larger exhibit into a smaller, traveling version and an online version. A memorabilia booklet, replete with quotations and timeline was prepared for the reception. Three major participants, Taylor Rodgers, a sanitation worker, Reverend Lawson, and William Lucy, now Secretary-Treasurer of AFSCME, were invited to speak at the event in a panel discussion regarding the strike and the civil rights movement. Picket signs were recreated and placed all around the exhibit space. The speakers noted that this was the first time they had been asked to speak publicly about the events of the 1968 Memphis Sanitation Strike and its aftermath.

The first online exhibit was created using Adobe Go Live, and launched six months after the physical exhibit was taken down. Photographs were limited to two to four on a Web page due to the fact that at the time most homes were still using dial-up connections. The text was significantly shortened, and panels were combined onto one page. In all, the initial online exhibit was nine Web pages in length, with separate pages for a bibliography and related links. Quotes also were included on some pages in an effort to try and recreate the emotional atmosphere of the physical exhibit. The scope of the online exhibit was extremely limited due to copyright restrictions and the ease with which material could be downloaded from the Internet. No news clippings were used; in fact, newspapers were not even contacted at that time. The archivists submitted their shortened exhibit to the Web designer and then lost intellectual control.

The original online exhibit was created without any thought given to the principles of information architecture, particularly those of usability and findability. In addition, there was little attention paid to the graphic design of the exhibit site. Unlike a Web site or a Web page, a virtual exhibit should create the same dynamic atmosphere as a physical exhibit. The fact that the format of the exhibit is electronic does not mean that it need be bland in nature. Indeed, virtual exhibits have the ability to be every bit as powerful as a physical exhibit.

The overall look of the 2003 online version is simplistic and visually unappealing. The text is black set against a plain white background. The

Figure 10.1   Screenshot of 2003 Virtual Exhibit.

Web designer opted for a vertical display, creating Web pages that forced users to scroll far down to read the entire text. The organizational structure was unclear since the navigation bar located at the bottom of each page contained different headings than those on the exhibit pages. Information on the home page was not centered, giving it a crowded look.

The rest of the exhibit, considerably shortened for the Internet, contained grammatical mistakes, did not have a timeline, and, due to the fear of copyright restrictions, did not include photographs that best represented the strike or the period in which it took place. There were no audio materials on the site, despite the fact that both audio and video materials from the reception symposium were available for use. The entire online exhibit was not a proper representation of the Memphis Sanitation Workers Strike or of the quality of materials contained in the collections at the Reuther Library. Moreover, the exhibit, with its static layout, didn't give the user any sense of the drama of the strike or the tensions, upheaval, and violence of the late 1960's.

I AM A MAN VERSION 2.0: REVAMPING
AN ONLINE EXHIBIT

Plans to create a new version of the online exhibit began in early March 2007. The fortieth anniversary of the strike was in 2008, and because of the new emerging technologies available through Web 2.0, it was a deemed the perfect time to re-evaluate and revise the exhibit to meet the current needs of scholars. The idea behind the creation of a new exhibit was to make it more user-centric, allowing users to comment and share information contained both at the Reuther Library and at other institutions. This had previously been done at the University of Michigan with its Polar Bear Expedition site[3] to great success. The Reuther Library decided to build upon that success and launch an exhibit that not only adhered to graphic design principles, but also allowed users to access information at their fingertips where they wanted, when they wanted—one of the central tenets of Web 2.0.

The traditional conception of a library or archive is one in which the services are one-directional: the users come to library to gather information. However, with Web 2.0, this is no longer the case. As Kevin Curran, Michelle Murray, and Martin Christian have pointed out, "The major difference between Library 1.0 and Library 2.0 (L2) is that Library 1.0 only allows for a one-way flow of information while L2 is a read-write library that gives library users the power to decide the service that they get."[4] The definition of Web 2.0 is still a source of debate, but it was first conceived by Tim O'Reilly as a set of applications that deliver a "continually-updated service that gets better the more people use it."[5]

Ellyssa Kroski defined Web 2.0 as "the evolution to a social and interactive Web that gives everyone a chance to participate."[6] She went on to note that "people are initiating incredible exchanges of knowledge through new Web tools that enable them to create, collaborate, socialize, and share [information]."[7] Thus, Web 2.0 allows users to gather information, discover the unexpected, and experience the creation of their peers. It also allows for continual interaction between the user and the institution. Bruce Dearstyne stated that Web 2.0 is "participatory, collaborative, inclusive, creator-user centric, unsettled, and very information intensive."[8]

Elizabeth Yakel put Web 2.0 in a specific archival context in an article written for *OCLC Systems and Services*. Here, she noted that, "Despite the early interest in using the Web to publicize their existence, services, and holdings, archives have been less experimental in recent years and slow to adopt some of the more interactive features that support social navigation."[9] The interactive tools of Web 2.0 force archivists to alter the relationship between themselves and scholars. Much of this reluctance to adopt these tools is due to the fact that archivists are afraid of losing intellectual control over the materials they hold in their repositories.

Yakel described social navigation, the main tool of Web 2.0 that archives can use to make themselves and their collections more accessible and user-friendly, as "situations in which one Web site visitor is aware of the previous visitors' navigational paths."[10] Users can create these navigational path through direct means, i.e., a blog or comment functionalities, or through indirect means, i.e. a recommender system.

Anne Goulding described Web 2.0 and libraries as "social capital", a term coined in the late 1980's by James Coleman. Social capital is "the relationships among persons, groups and communities, which engender trust and/or mutual obligations."[11] The trust in social capital, in turn, creates an environment that enables people to act more effectively and efficiently, thus making life more rewarding. For libraries, social capital is crucial since they are public spaces that foster a mutual and beneficial relationship between patron and librarian. Web 2.0 is the means by which libraries can create social capital and make themselves continually relevant in an ever-changing, technological world. As Curran, et al. pointed out, "Web 2.0's principles and technology offers libraries many opportunities to better serve their existing audiences and to reach out beyond the walls of the institution to reach potential beneficiaries where they happen to be, and in association with the task that they happen to be undertaking."[12]

With this in mind, the Reuther Library decided to revamp the I Am a Man exhibit. The library sought to push out valuable content and expertise where scholars could best benefit from it. Since one of the guiding principles of Web 2.0 is participation and feedback, the creators sought to create an exhibit that had the tools necessary for scholars and students to share information. After much exploration of various Web programs—both commercial and open source—the curators selected Macintosh's iWeb program. The Reuther Library's software and systems are built entirely upon a Mac platform, and the curators felt no need to step outside that platform and use a different program. The idea of hand coding the site was briefly discussed and considered, but ultimately rejected.

The first step in the creation process was to determine who exactly the various audiences would be. Based on previous usage of the Reuther Library's collection, it was decided that there were four potential groups of users for the exhibit, each with its own set of needs and technological skills. The first group was scholars: professors, Ph.D. candidates, and other graduate students. These individuals were primarily interested in Martin Luther King, Jr.'s assassination and role in the strike, AFSCME's role in the strike, Jerry Wurf (then President of AFSCME), and the civil rights, labor, and student protest movements. It was decided that most likely these scholars would skip over the exhibit entirely since they were already familiar with the course of events and go to the various downloadable documents, oral histories, and news clippings.

The second group was AFSCME members themselves, either those who had participated in the strike, or those who wanted to learn about the history of their union. AFSCME's Web site contains Martin Luther King's "I've Been to the Mountaintop" address and a timeline. Their main needs were the exhibit, the glossary and timeline of events, as well as a clear explanation of AFSCME's role in strike.

The third group, as defined by the curators, was students of all ages who would be looking at this event as a potential Black History Month project.

Their needs were the exhibit, photographs, biographical sketches of the main participants, a timeline, and a glossary.

The fourth group was archivists and librarians who might be looking at this exhibit as an example of how to create their own online exhibit using emerging technologies. They would most likely analyze how much information and how many documents we put online and would be most likely to contact the Webmaster and comment on exhibit, since they might have similar materials in their collections.

As a whole, one group—students—stood out as having very high technological skills. Scholars and archivists could have anywhere from high-to-low technological skills, while AFSCME members probably had little at all. Therefore, it was necessary to create an exhibit that was engaging enough for those with a high level of technological expertise, but one that also would be easily navigated by someone who did not often use the Internet.

After the audiences were clearly defined, it was necessary to determine which materials from the old exhibit would be used and which new materials would be added. It was obvious that in order to create an engaging, dynamic exhibit audio needed to be used throughout the exhibit. The archivists also decided, in an effort to make the exhibit more interactive, to include full-text documents. It was clear that to meet each user's needs, separate pages should be created for scholars, students, and teachers so that they could bypass the exhibit if necessary. Selection criteria for the documents, photographs, and audio for the virtual exhibit were the same as for a physical exhibit. Namely,

1. Does the material contribute to the narrative?
2. Are the photographs and audio engaging for the user?
3. Do the documents contribute to a greater understanding of the event?

Also, an added selection criterion for the scholars' page was: Are the documents useful and pertinent to scholarly research?

Since the initial virtual exhibit did not contain any documents, the archivists decided to search the AFSCME collections for any papers relating to the strike. After the materials were collected, the archivists weeded them according to the above criteria and the needs of the Web site. Documents were then scanned as a single page PDF that is easily downloadable, with one exception. The reception booklet containing a timeline and quotes was scanned as a multi-page PDF since this was merely informative rather than a primary source document.

Rather than cram panels together onto a Web page as had been done in the earlier online exhibit, the designers decided to create a separate page for each panel, which would also give the virtual exhibit the feeling of a physical exhibit. Two panels from the old online exhibit, "The Lorraine Motel" and "Memorial March", were taken out of the new exhibit since the current focus was specifically on the strike rather than on the participation of Martin Luther King, Jr. The archivists added a total of eight new panels: three to give background information on the situation in Memphis prior to 1968, one to illustrate how the community of Memphis responded, another to demonstrate the actions of AFSCME headquarters, and one to show how strikers tried to rally the city to their defense. Two panels were created from information crammed together in the old exhibit. Quotes were added from the symposium and other materials located in the collection (including audio), documents were added to certain exhibit panels, and photographs were chosen to give the audiences a more appropriate understanding of the strike.

iWeb is a sophisticated Web software program that allows for the easy creation of sophisticated Web pages. It uses a horizontal layout system with templates and cascading style sheets. Site organization and creation of a site map is easy to do and creators can simply cut and paste from previous pages so as to maintain consistency throughout the entire site. Media is easily added with the simple click of a button, as are hyperlinks, which may be anything from another Web site to a file stored on a server. Updating can also be done with the click of a button located at the bottom of the design toolbar. Once a decision was made regarding the software, the archivists began to layout the pages, first on paper, then on the computer.

The home page (http://www.reuther.wayne.edu/exhibits/iamaman/home.html) contained a banner of three photographs resized at 72 dpi for the Web. Across the photographs was placed a quote from Martin Luther King, Jr. in a bold, red font, to illustrate the tension and upheaval of the times. Centered directly underneath the banner, which would be used on every subsequent page (even those not directly in the exhibit), was a navigational toolbar that contained the following headings: About Us, Scholars, Teachers, Students, Related Links, and Comments. Located underneath this was the title of the page, "I Am A Man Virtual Exhibit", with a photograph of strikers bearing the trademark sign and a link to the exhibit with introductory text. If scholars wanted to bypass the exhibit they could do so simply by clicking on the "Scholars" link, which would take them directly to a list of documents and contact information. Located on the "Teachers" page is a curriculum for use during Black History Month, and contained in the "Students" page is a glossary, timeline, biographical sketches of important people, and documents. Photographs for download were not contained on these pages; instead users were instructed to contact the Library's audiovisual department.

Directly after the home page is the exhibit. Each page was laid out using the same format: banner, navigational tools (previous, next), panel title, photograph, text, quote (if applicable), home button, and navigational tools (previous, next). If audio was on a particular page, it was added next to the photograph. If documents were on the page, links to the files were placed directly underneath the informational text. Quotes were set off in italics,

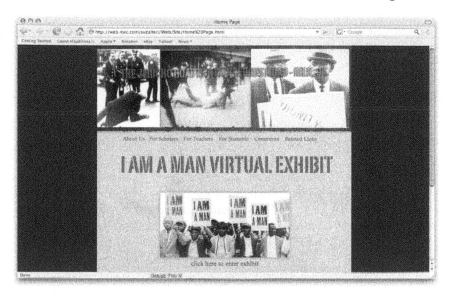

Figure 10.2   Screenshot of Current Exhibit.

and photographs contained descriptive captions as well as a credit if applicable. This layout made for a consistent, yet engaging exhibit. Panel titles were in a red font, while text was black set against a cream background. Document links were offset in a reddish tone, so users would know that they were hyperlinks to a file.

Audio from the symposium was transferred by the audio-visual department from a tape cassette into a MP3 format that could be downloaded onto a computer. After download, the exhibit creators used the open source audio editing program, Audacity, to cut, copy, and paste audio. They simply selected the part of the speech they wanted to use, and created a copy as a separate file. Once this was finished, exhibit designers could paste the new file onto a Web page by clicking on the Media button in the design toolbar of iWeb. The file is then transferred into a Quicktime file onto the Web page.

A comments section was added as a separate page. As Bruce Dearstyne has noted, blogs are "web journals that offer opinion and information that may include text, images, and links to other blogs and web sites."[13] Blogs can be made, as in the case of iWeb, to "have provisions for reactions and comments from users."[14] The blog is currently being used to post new information and updates from The Reuther Library as regards the exhibit. The blog also is being used by other institutions that post information about materials that they have, since information on this historic strike is scattered across academic institutions throughout the country. Finally, the blog is used to enhance communication among scholars, students, and participants. Comments posted to the blog have ranged from straightforward remarks to questions regarding where to locate specific materials, and opinions.[15] To make the blog more user friendly, we decided not to have users sign in and use passwords. That being said, we maintain control over the blog and can delete comments that are not appropriate for posting.

TESTING THE NEW EXHIBIT

After the comments section was completed, the archivists decided to beta test the exhibit among six people with varying backgrounds and technological skills. Three were archivists, one was a scholar from the scientific field, and two were former high school teachers. They were asked to answer the following questions:

1. Do all the links work? If no, please list those with problems.
2. Is the exhibit told in a narrative, chronological manner? Could the information be presented in a better manner? Was it easy to understand?
3. Did the audio function properly?
4. Did you feel there was too much information presented?
5. Did you have a difficult time navigating the site?
6. What do you think of the design of the site? Is everything presented in a clear and concise manner?
7. Do you have any other comments or suggestions?

Testers were given six hours to evaluate the Web site. They were given a Word document to fill out and return as soon as was possible for them. All testers noted that some of the links on the related links page were no longer functioning. All agreed the exhibit was presented well and had a logical, easy-to-follow presentation. One tester commented that the audio functioned in one browser and not the other. Those using old versions of Internet Explorer could not hear the audio because they did not have Quicktime. Two testers commented that the text could use some editing, and all testers documented PDFs that were illegible due to the age of the materials. One tester wanted the designers to add a separate panel dealing with the assassination of Martin Luther King, Jr.

Overall, the conclusion of the beta test was that the information was engaging and could be understood by all audiences. Minor mistakes regarding the scanning of PDFs were noted, and corrected, as were grammatical mistakes. It was important to test the site, not only to make sure the links worked, but to get an idea of how the site was used by individuals from different backgrounds who had varying degrees of technological expertise. One tester commented that if he could get through it, anyone could. After the mistakes were corrected, the site was republished with the changes.

CONCLUSION

For the academic researcher in history and the social sciences, the archive is essential. Primary source documents are the backbone for discovery and scholarship, but for many up-and-coming scholars, the archive conjures up images of restricted materials and stern-looking librarians and archivists. Since primary source materials are essential to scholarly research, the archival and librarian community must adjust their practices to meet the needs of their users. Digital access is essential for today's scholars.

A constant challenge to all archives, especially those dealing with social history, is to present materials in a way that engages users. More than half of Americans know little to nothing about what labor unions do. Nevertheless, the history of the American labor movement is synonymous with the development of our country. So how can an archive present this often forgotten and neglected history? Emerging technologies, such as social navigation and Web 2.0 offer the ability to enhance scholars' access to primary source materials. Since Web 2.0 requires the active participation of users through blogs and other arenas of participation, it has the potential to document the collective intelligence of users regarding a historical event. To that end, the Reuther Library created a revamped and enhanced virtual exhibit for the Memphis Sanitation Workers Strike of 1968. This exhibit has the potential to change not only the relationship between archivist and scholar and among users themselves. Researchers will now have the information they want, when they want, where they want. It remains to be seen whether their participation on the Web site leads to further scholarship trends.

NOTES

1. Katie Hafner, "History, Digitized (and Abridged)," *The New York Times*, March 11, 2007 http://query.nytimes.com/gst/fullpage.html?res=9500E5DC1331F932A25750C0A9619C8B63.
2. Martin Luther King, Jr. "I've Been to the Mountaintop," Mason Temple, Memphis, Tennessee, April 2, 1968.
3. University of Michigan, *Polar Bears Expedition Digital Collections*, January 1, 2005 http://polarbears.si.umich.edu. (May 20, 2007).
4. Kevin Curran, Michelle Murray and Christian Martin, "Taking the Information to the Public Through Library 2.0," *Library Hi Tech* 25 (2007): 288.
5. Ibid., 289.
6. Ellyssa Kroski, "The Social Tools of Web 2.0: Opportunities for Academic Libraries," *Choice* 44 (2007): 2011.
7. Ibid., 2011.
8. Bruce W. Dearstyne, "Blogs, Mashups & Wikis: Oh My!," *Information Management Journal* 41 (2007): 25.
9. Elizabeth Yakel, "Inviting the User into the Virtual Archives," *OCLC Systems & Services* 22 (2006): 159.
10. Ibid., 160.

11. Anne Goulding, "Editorial: Libraries and Social Capital," *Journal of Librarianship and Information Science* 36 (2004): 3.
12. Curran, et al., 296.
13. Dearstyne, 27.
14. Ibid., 27.
15. To see comments posted, visit http://www.reuther.wayne.edu/exhibits/iamaman/blog.html.

Contributors

Suzan A. Alteri, MLIS (Wayne State University) is the Social Sciences Librarian I at Purdy/Kresge Library, Wayne State University. Suzan Alteri was previously the American Federation of State, County and Municipal Employees Archivist at the Walter P. Reuther Library.

Ruth Bogan, MALS (Dominican University), is the Executive Director of PALS Plus, the Computer Consortium of Passaic County Libraries, Clifton, New Jersey.

Christine L. Borgman, PhD (Stanford University), **MLS** (University of Pittsburgh) is Professor and Presidential Chair in Information Studies at the University of California, Los Angeles. She is the author, most recently, of *Scholarship in the Digital Age: Information, Infrastructure, and the Internet* (MIT Press 2007).

James Bradley, MIS (Indiana University, Bloomington) is Head of Metadata and Digital Initiatives, Alexander M. Bracken Library, Ball State University. James Bradley was formerly Structured Text Specialist at the American Theological Library Association.

Delinda Stephens Buie, MLS (University of Kentucky) is Professor and Curator of Rare Books, Special Collections, William F. Ekstrom Library, University of Louisville.

Daniel D. Golodner, MLIS (Wayne State University) is the American Federation of Teachers Archivist (Archivist III) at the Walter P. Reuther Library, Wayne State University.

Margaret E. Hale, MSLIS (Simmons College, Boston, MA) is the Librarian for Collections Digitization at the Harvard College Library, Widener Library, Harvard University.

Rachel I. Howard, MLIS (University of Washington) is Assistant Professor and Digital Initiatives Librarian, William F. Ekstrom Library, University of Louisville.

Richard Lesage, MTh (Centre Sèvres—Facultés jésuites de Paris, France), **MSLIS** (Simmons College, Boston, MA), is the Digital Projects Librarian at the Harvard College Library, Widener Library, Harvard University.

Diane Maher, MA (San Diego State University), **MLS** (University of California–Los Angeles), is the University Archivist at the Copley Library, University of San Diego.

Alla Makeeva-Roylance is an award-winning librarian and a freelance translator of Polish and Russian. Her primary areas of interest are history and literature, and her translations have been published in the USA and Poland.

Shawn Martin, MA (College of William and Mary) is Scholarly Communication Librarian, Van Pelt Library, University of Pennsylvania. Previously, Shawn was Text Creation Partnership Project Librarian at the University of Michigan, and he currently serves as executive director of the American Association for History and Computing.

Albina Moscicka, PhD (Institute of Geodesdy and Cartography) is a tutor in the Department of Cartography, Institute of Geodesy and Cartography,Warsaw, Poland.

Elena García-Puente, BA (Universidad Complutense de Madrid) is Head of the Serials Bibliographic Control Service of the National Library of Spain, Madrid.

Amy Hanaford Purcell, BA (University of Kentucky) is Associate Curator, Special Collections, William F. Ekstrom Library, University of Louisville.

Lola Rodríguez, BA (Universidad Complutense de Madrid) is Head of the Serials Collection Management Service of the National Library of Spain, Madrid.

Bradley L. Schaffner, MA, MLS (Indiana University, Bloomington) is Head of the Slavic Division of Widener Library of the Harvard College Library, Slavic Division, Widener Library, Harvard University.

Susan Schreibman, PhD (University College, Dublin, Ireland) is Director, Digital Humanities Observatory, Royal Irish Academy, Dublin, Ireland.

Edward D. Starkey, MA (University of Dayton), **MSLS** (University of Kentucky) is the University Librarian at the Copley Library, University of San Diego.

John B. Straw, MLS (Indiana University) is Assistant Dean for Digital Initiatives and Special Collections, Ball State University Libraries.

Jennifer A. Younger, MALS, PhD (University of Wisconsin–Madison) is the Edward H. Arnold Director of University Libraries at the University Libraries, University of Notre Dame.

Index

Milton Keynes UK
Ingram Content Group UK Ltd.
UKHW031134141024
449569UK00006B/198